SPAGHETTI WITH A SAWED-OFF SHOTGUN

By

R. R. Vigorelli

First Edition.

ISBN 978-0-578-11072-1

FOREWORD

This book is both about my life and about everything that I have learned. It is not intended to hurt anyone or to make anyone look particularly bad. I decided to write it because I have some good stories to tell and maybe I can help someone out by preventing the same things from happening again.

The book is divided into sections of my life with the last section serving as a wrap up during my time in Los Angeles. This is as much my story as it is anyone else's. This is not a "tell-all" book; I have left a lot of things out mostly for the sake of brevity. I have limited the names of the people that appear in my book for legal and personal reasons, along with the names of several companies. There are some very strange things in this book, and I swear it is all true.

HORNS AND HALOS

When I was a kid in Sandy, Utah my mom would take me and my sister to church with every Sunday. As a toddler I was placed in the nursery while my mom attended her Bible study classes. I was a very happy kid; I almost always had a smile on my face. Whenever I would meet somebody new especially another baby I would walk up to them, give them a big hug and say, "Hi, my name is Ricky. What's yours?" One special day in the church nursery I met another baby, and I introduced myself like I always do. I was expecting to make a new friend. Ten seconds later I was on my well-diapered ass with a stinging red mark on my cheek, and a very grumpy looking two-year-old staring down at me. I was only two-some-odd years old and I had just gotten bitch-slapped by another baby. My friend B. S. who was just a little older than me looked at me like, "Dude you gonna hit him back?" So I did what any self-respecting child of that age would do—I cried like the baby that I was. I mean what the hell, I was just trying to be nice and this jerk decks me in front of God and everybody and in a church no less. I learned very early on that some people just have no class. So the nannies came over and separated us. I got coddled and my assailant got a good talking to and a time out. To the best of my knowledge I never saw that person again.

When I was 4 I had these blue synthetic pants that I loved. They were light blue and had a white stripe down the side of either leg. This white stripe was in turn bordered by a raised line of red material on either side.

To a four-year-old these were the coolest pants ever. One summer's day I was wearing these pants. Now one of the things you have to understand about Utah is that it gets really hot there in the summer, so it was probably early to mid-June. It was warm enough that I didn't need a jacket, but cool enough that I didn't need to drop down to shorts. It was probably late afternoon, and I was playing with the neighbor kids. I don't remember exactly what we were playing, but I thought it was a stupid game. Everybody else seemed to be enjoying themselves except me. So I went home a little depressed. I walked into the back yard through the garage; it was actually an overbuilt carport, but we called it a garage. I sat down on the stairs to our back deck while I watched my dad push what I thought was this loud and dirty machine over the grass. A few years later I learned that the monstrous machine that my dad was using was our 1980-something orange and white Jorgensen lawn mower that guzzled a gallon of gas for the front and back yards each to mow. Ain't we come we come along way? I watched as my dad finished the lawn and bagged the grass. He then looked up and saw me sitting there and said, "Hey Bear, what's up? Why aren't you with your friends?"

"They were playing a dumb game for babies. I was bored. So I came home. I don't really think that I fit in."

"Oh c'mon, I'm sure you fit in just fine."

I looked down at my pants and said, "I feel like I'm too old to play with them Daddy. I've always felt this way, and I don't know why. I don't like playing with the other kids."

My dad stopped and stared at me for a minute. Then he said, "That's okay. I want you to go inside and wash up for dinner. And tell Mommy that I will be in in a few minutes, okay?"

"Okay."

My dad then patted me on the shoulder and gave me a big sweaty hug and I went inside the house.

In the Mormon Church when a child turns eight, he or she is baptized into the Church and their formal education on the gospel begins. All of my friends at church and school were getting baptized, and I was getting really excited because my birthday was coming up and that meant that I was going to get baptized. Except that I didn't get baptized. You see, my dad is Catholic and he doesn't really like the Mormon Church that much, which is kind of strange because he married my mother who is, or at least was at the time, Mormon. My dad said that I was too young to get baptized into a religion that I, in his opinion, knew nothing about. He wanted me to be old enough and wise enough to make my own choice in matters relating to God. I found out later that he didn't care what religion I became part of as long as it was my good and honest choice and based on reason not societal pressure. And he really didn't like Mormons.

Even though I didn't get baptized I did get something that every kid wants—a video game console. My parents got me a Genesis. For those of you who think that video games have only been around since the PS 1, think again. The Genesis was the fourth generation of gaming, and contained a monumental 8 bits of processing power.

I wanted some kind of video game thing for as long as I knew what they were, and I got my first one when I was eight. Looking back I see it now as payment for what happened later. Let me explain. In the sect of Mormonism that I grew up in, they are very concerned with purity. I was considered "impure". In a week's time I went from nearly the entire Ward—a Ward is a local designation within the Church similar to a Parish the next level up is Stake which is like a Diocese—loving me and treating me like their golden boy to almost no one talking to me or my mom. My sister had already moved away for college so she no longer mattered to them—she was regarded as dead. This was all because I hadn't been baptized on time.

At the time I didn't understand what had happened, and I really didn't care. I was still part of the local scout troop that was funded by the Church, and I was having a great time of it. I still went to church and studied and participated and had a great time of it. But for some reason I was treated like a stray animal, rather than as a person. Then a few weeks later a returned missionary came up to me and we started talking. He was tall, which to me was huge. He had blonde hair that was cut very short and styled impeccably with gel. He had very light piercing blue eyes. He was actually as beautiful as a young man can be. As the conversation took shape, he started quoting scripture and he said to me that people with dark hair, dark eyes and dark skin like mine were cursed by God because their great-grand parents had turned away from God, so now I was lesser in the Eyes of God. He went on to say that if I wanted to get into Heaven and meet Jesus that I would have to work twice as hard as everyone else and then maybe God would find me worthy enough to be allowed into Heaven.

This devastated me. I was so depressed, and nothing anybody said or did could bring me out for weeks. Because he was a missionary, and therefore a "good person" who "spoke for God", I believed what he had said, but I never told anyone for years afterward. As a result, I didn't trust anyone with blonde hair and blue eyes for years, and until I was 22 I didn't identify myself as white. I didn't know what I was, other than Italian, but I knew I wasn't white. So on all the government forms that I had to fill out in school I marked "other".

My eighth birthday was a huge turning point in my life socially speaking. Slowly all of my friends drifted away from me, until at best I had acquaintances at school that would talk to me if they had time or needed something from me. I learned very early what racism was and what bigotry was, and I got the full force.

When I was 11 or 12, I was asked to give a talk in sacrament meeting about the importance of tithing. Tithing in Mormonism is giving money to the Church as an offering. A minimum 10 percent is required to be given from all forms of gross income. That means off the top not the bottom line, and it is tracked. Now there is a law in Heaven that says we must give of ourselves to attain enlightenment. At the time, I did not know any of this. All I knew was we had to give money to the Church so we could get blessings from God. So for my talk on tithing I did some research. We had just barely gotten a computer and the internet at my house and I loved it. I researched tithing and what it has been to so many different religions throughout history. I gave my findings in sacrament meeting and people were stunned. They never knew that our church was not the first to require an offering of some kind. I cited Genesis with Cain and Abel and called that non-monetary tithing. I had been told to give a talk on tithing, and what I decided to do was to say that every single one of God's children is required to give. I wanted people to understand that just because the times may change the law will not. Oddly no one spoke to me for the rest of the day, and I was never asked to give a talk again.

During the summer when I was 12 I got the opportunity to go on a week-long camping trip with my scout troop. There was no chance of rain, so there was no chance of them wussing out, which was actually a big problem. Whenever the scout master wanted to take us out on a camping trip he got scared of a tiny bit of rain; even if it was only enough to cut the dust. He would get us all set up and then cancel at the last minute. My dad would even volunteer to take us out, but because he was a heathen of a Catholic he was banned from even our most rudimentary meetings much less a campout. So when this big campout came around I went. I really shouldn't have done that. There was an entrance fee of $200, which covered food and fuel. When we got there, we then had to pay five bucks for each merit badge in order to participate.

It was a gorgeous place though; it was a full legal running mass camp in the Uinta National Forest which is high alpine terrain. Since I couldn't afford the badges I decided to make the best of it and hang out at our campsite. I took nice long naps in the sun while slung up in a hammock. I even made friends with some chipmunks. About halfway through the campout some of the guys in the troop decided to go fishing in the lake by the campsite. I told them to go ahead and I would find them eventually, so they took off. I went off to find them and I couldn't do it. This was because I got lost. I thought I was at one place when I was actually somewhere else entirely.

And then I pooped my pants. I was trying to hold it and find one of the port-a-potties that I had just passed. I was sweating and doing everything I could to keep from letting it go, and then it happened. It was very embarrassing. When I finally got back to camp, I changed and skunked away in shame.

The next day I almost drowned. That might be a bit of a stretch. One of my friends in the troop wanted to earn a badge for rowing. He asked me if I would be good enough to help him and I said sure. So we jumped in a row boat and he paddled out to the center of the lake. He then secured the oar inside the boat and started rocking it. I asked him just what the hell he thought he was doing and he didn't answer me. Ten seconds later we capsized. I surfaced under the boat in near total darkness. When I realized where I was, I managed to get out from under the boat and re-surface before that idiot righted the boat. When I saw him I chewed him out. He acted completely innocent and said that it was part of the badge. I wanted to hit him. When we got back to the dock I stomped off and returned to the camp to sit by the fire. It took me nearly 2 days to dry out because I didn't bring another change of clothes. Despite the natural beauty of the camp, I had a horrible time. As soon as I got home and showered for about an hour, I decided that I was done with scouts forever. I didn't as much quit as I just stopped showing up. I can't tell you how much money and time that saved me. After all, my entire troop was a bunch of girly-men that only wanted to play basketball.

After I graduated from grade school to middle school, I was given a chance to re-invent myself. I started middle school and started making new friends. I was very careful to not let them in on my secrets at all. As far as anyone knew I was just a regular kid that happened to be growing facial hair. With the Church I was now beginning to prove my worth to them. One of the home teachers recommended me for baptism. The Church has an office within its ranks called "home teacher". These people show up at your door often unannounced to just see how things are going, make sure everything is okay, and to be a good neighbor. Local missionaries were called to come teach me about the Church. Just because I had been Mormon since I was a baby didn't actually mean anything, everybody has to go through the discussions as they are called.

When the 2 missionaries and the 2 home teachers pulled up, one of the missionaries said to my home teacher, "There is no way this kid knows enough to be baptized. He can't be ready." They came into my home and started asking me questions about the Bible and the Book of Mormon. Not only did I get the questions right—I went into correlative detail about the stories. I gave them information that most people only know if they have been studying the scriptures for years, which I had been doing. I find religion fascinating. When the 4 men had left, I heard one of them say as they were going out to the car, “He’s ready.”

So for the next 2 weeks or so I was fast-tracked through the discussions and the training for the ceremony. I was baptized at the age of 13 by a dear friend of the family who was also my former bishop. I wasn’t too crazy about the outfit, however. It was a white polyester jumpsuit that had bell bottom style legs and hugged the crotch a little too closely. I looked like Elvis minus the rhinestones, cape and drug problem. I guess they couldn’t afford to update the ceremonial styles even though the Church is worth billions. Whatever, I was too excited to care. My dad had finally let me be baptized. The Church was permitting me to be included in their society. I finally felt like I was a person, and it felt good.

I was led to the font which was at one end of a large viewing room. The pool itself was set with some beautiful if however modest blue tile. The water was warm and inviting. I stepped in and the viewing doors were pulled open. I could see my all my family and friends who were in attendance. Wow was I nervous. Everybody was there that I had wanted to be there. All that I hoped for was that I went completely under when I was dunked. It was an issue because if I didn’t go completely under it meant that God had rejected me and we would have to try again and again until I was completely under. My baptizer then took me by the arm and spoke the prayer. My nose was plugged and I was bent over backwards submerging me into the pool of water. Before I really had time to realize what had happened, I was brought back up out of the water.

I asked, “Did I do it?”

My baptizer replied, "You made it. You went completely under, and came up perfectly."

I was confirmed as a full member of the Church of Jesus Christ of Latter Day Saints (Mormon) the following Sunday. Then a week later I was made a deacon in the Aaronic Priesthood, which is the lowest level of rank for priesthood holders. It is given to males aged 12 years and older and allows them to serve the sacrament (communion) to the parishioners, to collect fast offerings on Fast Sunday. A "fast offering" is the amount of money that one would use to buy a meal. Mormons are not supposed to eat at least one meal on the first Sunday of every month as a reminder that some people are starving. It is a day that is supposed to be devoted to prayer and careful study. The idea is to build one's relationship with the divine, and to sacrifice earthly growth for spiritual growth. I was elated to be able to do this work of collecting the offerings. I felt great. I felt like I was welcomed again in my own religion, and everybody treated me as such.

A few months later around my fourteenth birthday, I was made a teacher in the Aaronic Priesthood. The roll of the teacher is the same as a deacon with one addition: I was now able to go out into the local church community as a home teacher. During the time between becoming a deacon and becoming a teacher, I passed out the sacrament to the people every Sunday. Once a month I went around the neighborhood to collect the fast offerings. When I became a teacher I continued with the knowledge that if I was activated as a home teacher I would be compelled to do the job, and I was excited about it.

Then cracks started to develop. I started taking harder classes at school and working after class. I realized that if I wanted to still ace all my classes and maintain a social life I would have to cut something out. I only have so much energy. So, I pulled back on my church duties and stopped going as often in favor of actually doing my homework and helping around the house. When I didn't show up for a few weeks to church my bishop called me and requested that I come see him at my nearest convenience. I obliged, and met with him the following Sunday. He asked me how everything was at home, and if I was doing okay. I said everything was fine; my classes were a little more intense and I was working so I had to make some schedule cuts and 3 hours of church versus 3 hours of study time seemed like a fair trade. I told him that I would come to church when I could and I would do all that I could, but school came first. My bishop agreed and asked if he could see me once every 6 months or so just to see how I was doing. I said sure no problem.

The next 2 years went very well with me and the Church. During the school year I would go to church when I could, and during the summer I was there just about every week as I had promised. When I turned 16 I advanced in rank to become a priest. This meant that I was now able to bless the sacrament as well as pass it. My bishop offered me some callings within the church (jobs)—I politely turned them down do to scheduling conflicts. I had less time to play with now that my classes were more intense as was my home life and my social life. My bishop said that was "unfortunate" and that I would never advance in the Church if I didn't do as he recommended. I said I would look things over and get back to him in a month. So I set up an appointment with him, we shook hands and I left.

I returned a month later for our appointment. I was dressed in some old jeans and a t-shirt. I was exhausted from everything that I had done that week. I was 5 or 10 minutes early for the appointment. The bishop's clerk/secretary said he would be with me shortly. So I took a seat outside of the chapel to wait. I waited for 30 minutes. He then came out and got me and pulled me into his office. He apologized for making me wait; the person he was talking to needed some extra counseling, and it was an isolated incident. Fine. We talked. He asked me how things were going: parents, school work, girls, etc. Everything was fine, just a little stressful. I told him I would not be able to take on the added responsibilities of a calling. Again that was unfortunate. He then proceeded to lecture me on morality and my place in the Church, most of which I tuned out as dribble. I would check in every so often to make it look like I was paying attention. The technique had served me well in the past why not now? It worked perfectly. After I left my meeting with the bishop, I was not in a good mood. I went to my room turned up my radio and started reading for my classes the next day.

After that day every 4 to 6 months the bishop would call me at home and request my presence in a meeting with him, and like an idiot I always said yes. I say "idiot" because every time I would go for a meeting he would waste about 30 minutes to an hour of my time talking with a person "because the Spirit was needing to talk". This was time that I could have used on studying or reading or sitting with my cat or my family. Eventually I got so fed up with him that day I gave him 10 minutes after our appointment time. This is still rather generous; I am a generous man after all. At the end of the time I left. Just as I got home he called me and apologized. It was everything I could do to keep from screaming at him over the phone. He asked if he could see me again another time—I said I would get back to him on that.

I'm sure you are wondering why I would ever do that to someone who had wasted my time like that. Why would I ever treat someone kindly who had treated me so poorly? I have a few reasons. First, as Jesus said, "Turn the other cheek." Second, the bishop out ranked me. You see, the Mormon Church is set up in a system resembling the military; it makes things very efficient and very clear. Finally, I knew if I did tell him off I would be lucky if all the Church decided to do to me was excommunicate me. So as an act of rebellion, I just stopped going to church. My mom and I stopped opening the front door when the boys came collecting fast offerings on Sunday.

Things were great. My confidence started to improve. I even started to date more often. I met a girl at the start of my junior year who would prove to be very dangerous and destructive not only to me but to everything in my life including my relationship with the Divine. I will go into that story later. When I was finally released from her clutches, I started going back to church. I even registered for Seminary. Seminary is release time from the school for a class period during the day. During this time students may legally leave school grounds to go home or go to the church located off campus for religious i.e. Mormon studies. Previously, I had never registered for Seminary. My parents and I believed it to be unnecessary and a waste of class credits, but now with a big gaping hole in my soul I needed something.

I went for the first level of Seminary. Yes there are levels, four to be exact. My bishop was very proud of me, even though he seemed to be talking to me like I had deserved the hell that I had just gone through. I went to Seminary for the first two times, felt depressed, skipped the third and got kicked out. So I quit going to church again all together. I instead started reading on my own, and not just the Bible. I picked up Zen Buddhism, Wicca, the Taoist art of Feng Shui, general Paganism including divination and astrology. Over the next 4 or 5 years I began to realize that I had been lied to. I started finding fault with the Church. I began to re-interpret everything that I had read and been told on an empirical basis. By the time I had graduated from high school I had gone from true-believer to lip-server.

The strangest part was this however: I would go to church when it suited me, and as a result I was able to secure my rank of elder by the time I was nineteen. It was a year late but I knew through my studies of energetics that it might come in handy. Obtaining the rank was rather difficult however. My bishop stonewalled me. He said that I had to prove my worthiness to him before he would allow me to receive this advanced rank. Elder is considered advanced because it is not part of the Aaronic Priesthood, it is the Melchizedek Priesthood. It is the same level as the Church's President/Prophet. Assuming everything that I had been told was truthful, this rank would be some pretty powerful stuff. I would be able to heal the sick and wounded, cast out evil spirits, and speak directly with God. I attempted to change wards without moving, because my bishop and I didn't exactly get along. That was impossible. You see in Mormonism, unlike other forms of Christianity, you go to church where you are told to go and it's based on where you live. It's meant to be easy and convenient. However to someone who is at odds with the Church it's just another form of control from a perceived enemy.

So I played the bishop's game. I became a home teacher and I made some friends. I started to think maybe this Church ain't so bad. Maybe I can be happy. After I gained my rank as elder, I started wanting to date again. So I started going to the single's ward at Westminster College where I was doing my undergrad. A single's ward is for people, usually young adults that are unmarried. The idea is to get them to meet and mingle and date and marry, because the unofficial stand of the Church is "an unmarried person is a menace to society". I picked the one at Westminster even though I didn't live anywhere near it because the girls at Westminster were gorgeous. I loved that school. The eye candy alone was worth the 10 grand a semester, but I digress. Attempting to transfer was a huge mistake. My bishop called me into his office and effectively tore me a new one. How dare I try to leave my home ward—again!

Then he asked me if I had considered going on a mission. I had considered it, but I wasn't decided. On one hand I had the inherent spiritual advancement that results from a monastic life. On the other hand I had my education, which was a full ride scholarship to one of the best schools in not only the state but the country. My family is proud but not great. In Utah we are considered second class, so I don't have my name to fall back on. I grew up poor and my education was my only hope for any kind of future. If I left for a mission I would forfeit my scholarship and loose any chance of a prosperous future ever. I told my bishop I would talk to God about it and get back to him later.

That night I went into meditation and prayer. I asked God if I should go on a mission, this was the answer: "You are not normal. You have never been normal. You will never be normal. Stop trying to be normal, and just be who you are meant to be."

I came out of meditation with my answer, and chose school and I paid a huge price for it. When I met with my bishop again I told him that I would be continuing with my education and not going on a mission. When he asked me why, I lied and said that my father would disown me if I went. In all reality my dad wouldn't have agreed to the idea of a mission, but I would still be part of the family. My bishop seemed to understand, but he did say that if I didn't go I "would have to bear in mind the consequences of my choice".

"Consequences? I thought that it was my choice. What about my free agency to determine my own destiny?"

"Oh you still have that. But you do have to bear in mind the consequences of everything you do."

I took that as a threat. I have never seen that statement in anything that I have read, seen, or watched where that was only constructive criticism and not a threat.

Then he asked me about my tithing; which was something that I had always been at odds with. He asked me how much money I was making and why I was only paying $5 a month. He knew I had to be making more. I told him that had bills, and $5 was all I could spare. He asked me if I was aware of the commandment of tithing, but he asked like if I was aware that if a played with a match in a dry forest that I would burn it down. I was keenly aware of it. He then demanded to see my financial records from the past year in order to verify that I was paying the proper amount and if I wasn't how much I owed. In 5 minutes my bishop had turned something was supposed to be charity into a tax or even a fee for worship. I was very unhappy. I told him my records were my own business, and I left.

I started going exclusively to the Westminster singles ward hoping for some solace. I found none. Nobody would even look at me. Whenever I went to church I got depressed to the point of being borderline suicidal. I didn't date. I didn't go out. I didn't do anything except go to work, go to school and spend time at home. I literally hated everything, because everything I saw I felt was literally owned by the Church in some way. I did eventually break from the Church. As to how I did it—that is a story for later in this book, it's kind of neat.

FAMILY (NOUN): CRAZY ITALIANS AND MORMONIZED GYPSIES

I want to make something clear before I begin. I love my family. They are my blood. They are my kin. No matter what certain individuals may have done, are doing or will do in the future I will always have a large place in my heart for my family. And no one can take that away.

I was born in a suburb of Salt Lake City, Utah called Murray. It was raining hard on October 10, 1983. My mom started having contractions early in the morning, so her and my dad jumped into a beat up Oldsmobile Cutlass that was a bit of a boat and punched it to Murray from our place in Sandy. Why Murray? The hospital in Sandy hadn't been built yet. They had to make a trip of about 6 miles as fast as possible in freezing rain. They made it just fine.

I was delivered a little after 8 AM, and only a few moments after my birth my tiny hand reached up and touched my left cheek just under my eye. When I pulled back a big red mark had appeared where my hand had been. My scar as I call it has been the source of many questions about my mental stability, preclusion to fights, beatings, and even my being human. For the most part it is just a birth mark, and I wear it proudly to this day despite numerous cosmetic surgeons wanting to remove it.

When my dad got all the confirmations of my health and was able to make it to a pay phone he started making calls to our family. His brothers, sisters and my grandma, his mom, were overjoyed. The Italian side of my family was so happy to welcome another boy into the family; the joy would have been the same even if I was a girl. My mom's family was a different story. Two of her sisters were as happy as was my grandma. Her third sister and her father, my grandpa, were not happy per se. This sister and my mom had some bad blood, so anything good that happened to my mom was an insult to the sister. My grandpa is quoted by my dad as saying, "Are you sure? I was expecting a girl." I could already feel the love. To my grandpa men are superior to women. So when my mom, his least favorite daughter gave birth to a son his logic centers changed. The gender roles in many parts of Utah are very strange. Men are just seen as being stupid brutes that only know how to kill or impregnate, yet women are only good for making babies and keeping the house nice and giving her husband something to hit. Yeah I know it makes no sense to me either.

Now because of this my mom's mom, my grandmother, gave me 2 very strange gifts in my first year. The first was my christening gown, which was actually a very pretty dress; and the second was purple footy pajamas in the shape of a bunny rabbit like on that Christmas movie. It was a little embarrassing, but I think it's funny as hell now. In my grandma's defense, she had never bought anything for a boy and didn't quite know what the opposite things to do for a girl would be so she guessed—she was wrong. As a result of this she did her best to make up for it later in my life and she succeeded. I honor her memory every day. God rest her.

As a baby, like I said before, I was so happy. Unless of course my physical needs required tending to or I was scared about something. I loved to play, especially with my daddy. It started off with pica boo and later evolved to tickling a chasing and wrestling as I got older. My dad's brothers were fun too, and would often serve as a good substitute for my dad when we were in Price for a visit. I liked them because they looked a lot like my dad. I actually thought they were clones or something.

I can actually remember an instance with one of my cousins during an Easter visit. She was very Italian; basically everything must be Italian or it's no good. What can I say, we're a proud people. I can remember her playing pica boo with me using a blanket to cover me so I was hidden. She would then say, "Where did Ricky go? Where's Ricky?" I would start to giggle. Then the blanket would come off me and she would say, "Oh my, it's a little Italian baby!" I belly laughed. I was only few months old sitting up and trying to walk at the time, but my laughter could fill a home and rattle pictures on the wall. Not an exaggeration.

I have a lot of really fond memories of holidays and gatherings with my Italian family. There is a key piece of difference between them and my immediate home. In my house we were very quiet. TV and radio were kept low, and yelling or shouting were only done when necessary. The rest of my dad's family on the other hand...well we're Italian, we're loud and we talk with our hands. The more of us that get together in an area the louder and more gestury we become. Now I find it great and inviting, as a baby who wasn't quite used to it, the noise and commotion was a little jarring for a couple of hours until I realized where I was. I'm sure you're wondering why Italians need to use their hands so much. The answer is that's just how we talk. When John Gotti was arrested he didn't say much because he couldn't. His hands were cuffed behind his back, half of how he spoke was gone, and my family and I are no different.

Where my dad's family is warm, vibrant and action oriented my mom's family is cold, reserved and meticulous. These two families are almost polar opposites. The title of this section is "Crazy Italians and Mormonized Gypsies". That is not entirely accurate. Yes, from my maternal grandmother who is Romanian there is some Gypsy in there, it's not much but as my grandpa would say, "a fly in the ointment is still a fly in the ointment". As a result of this view from my grandpa I am one of the few members of the family that identifies at all with the Romanian much less the Gypsy side of the family. The rest consider themselves to be Irish-German as my grandpa is.

Get-togethers with my mom's side of the family were always…calm for lack of a better word. Music was the center of the family as was the Mormon Church. My grandma was a Julliard graduate and actually sang in the Tabernacle Choir for many years. Everyone in the family can play at least one musical instrument, except for my sister and myself. My sister started to learn to play the piano but quickly lost interest after about a year or so. I tried to learn, but my hands were too small and my grandma/teacher would crush instead of press my fingers against the keys causing pain. Thus I equated music with pain and thus I said not only "no" but "hell no" to learning to not only any instrument but to singing as well. To this day I will only sing if it is with the radio or I'm drunk.

My dad has always been a big part of my life. As a baby, I played with my dad a lot. I loved to walk up his chest and then have him pick me up and hold me all the way up so the ceiling so I could touch it. To a two-year-old that is the coolest thing since cartoons. As an infant, my dad would watch me while my mom went to work at a local steakhouse. Now as I said I loved to play with my daddy. And one of my favorite games/tricks to play on him was the gross game. The object of the game was how can I gross my daddy out the most and therefore have the most fun. A sure fire move was to poop myself just after mommy left. Now when I say "poop" I do not mean a little candy bar looking thing in the diaper, no no. I mean outside the diaper and up the back. One of the big reasons I used to do it was liked how it felt on my skin; it was warm and goopy, and what baby or kid doesn't like warm goopy things.

On this particular day my mom had just given me a bath and put me in clean clothes. I was cute as a button. As she was leaving she made a point to tell my dad to make sure I stayed clean and she would be back in a few minutes. Then she left. Hehe show time. Ten seconds after the door closed my dad looked at me and noticed my face was a little red. "Oh no. Don't you dare. Don't you dare poop."

I pooped.

It was perfect. It went all the way up the back and my daddy was freaking out. He picked me up and rushed me into the bathroom. All part of the game, and I was having a blast. He stripped me down and started hosing me off. There was poo everywhere! I won! My dad got me cleaned up and did a load of laundry. Everything was clean by the time my mom got home. My dad had thought of everything except for a teeny, tiny detail. He had dressed me in different clothes, and my mom noticed. It was like a scene from a sitcom, my day was complete.

About a year later, my dad had learned to kind of watch me. Babies are always into something, so on days where my dad had to do maintenance on his truck and my mom wasn't around to tend me he would take outside and let me help. By "help" I mean I sat on his chest and had fun while watching him work. One particular day the summer before I turned 2 we were changing the oil on my dad's truck while my mom was at work. The old oil was drained, and the new oil was being put in. I got a little bored and wandered into the backyard. My dad had placed the old oil back there to keep me out of it. Out of sight, out of mind. That usually works except for one thing, I can't be tricked. I found the oil sat down and started playing with it. I eventually picked up the whole pan and poured it over my head and coated my entire body with it. There was no place I didn't have oil. My dad's heart about stopped when he found me due to the sound of the metal oil pan hitting the brick patio just beside me. My mom would be home in about thirty-some-odd minutes and of course I was supposed to stay clean. I loved messing with my dad. He scooped me up and rushed me to the bathroom in the house. I was wearing a white t-shirt—now black and a white diaper—also now black. The oil had found its way into everything on my body. My dad stripped me down and plunked me in the tub. I got scrubbed down and my oily clothes got thrown out. My dad finished with me and sat me down in the living room to play just as my mom walked in the front door.

"There's my guys. So what did you do today?"

"Oh you know, we played went outside. Guy stuff."

Then my mom touched my head. She pulled her hand back and showed it to my dad. "What's this?"

It was covered in oil. My dad had failed to wash my hair. He got in trouble.

Dad would take me out fishing and camping a lot during the hot Utah summers. My mom and sister came along also, but my main focus was my dad. One time when I was 3 or so, I got my first fishing pole. It was one of those little plastic things that you buy in the sport shop so the kid can have something to do while everyone is at the lake or whatever. I watched my dad thread a worm into his hook and then he threaded one onto mine. He gave me my pole back and told me to hold still while he casted his pole. He then took my pole and casted mine after he showed me how. He told me to hold onto the pole until I felt something try to pull it out of my hands. So, I'm this little kid about two-and-a-half feet tall standing on the bank of a reservoir called Red Creek—or "crick" as Utahns call it—holding a tiny fishing pole in my tiny hands. I felt so big.

Then something really weird happened. I felt a tug. I set my pole down and ran over to my dad and showed him what was happening. The pole was slowly moving into the water with every tug. My dad grabbed the pole and started turning the reel. He yelled back to my mom, "Linda! Ricky caught a fish!" So my mom and sister ran over to see. My dad reeled in a good 5 pounder for me. He took the hook out of its mouth and showed me my catch. We were all very excited, and I guess I got a little carried away because I grabbed the fish with my bare hands and kissed it on the mouth. No joke. In my defense, I was 3 and most of my knowledge of the outside world consisted of cartoons, and whenever I saw a person catch a fish in a cartoon they kissed it. That grossed my sister out a little bit to say the least. We actually ate that fish a few nights later and I was very proud to have gotten dinner for my family.

As I got older, when we would go fishing I didn't have as good of a time. I would get bored and start throwing rocks in the water because I liked the kurplunk sound they made. My dad did not like this. He would always tell me, "Ricky, don't throw rocks. Hey stop throwing rocks." He always said it as if I would listen. But he would always catch a fish after I threw about 3 rocks in. I stirred up the fish and one would invariably snag itself on the hook. I do tend to think outside the box.

One of the most pleasant and comforting smells that to me is the smell of pine logs on a campfire. Let me explain. Aside from fishing, my dad loved to take the family camping. We had a huge tent capable of sleeping 6 people. We would take this tent up to the forest near

Red Creek or into the Uinta Mountains as long as the weather was okay. We would use dead fall logs usually pine and cook our meals with the campfire. The food wasn't that great but that's not the point. Getting out of the city was wonderful, and for being from the small city that I am you can imagine what a big city does to me.

It was on one of these trips that my dad gave me my nickname; by the way he is the only one allowed to use it. I was probably a toddler and we decided to go camping up in the Uintas. The woods on these mountain sides are thick, dark pine forests known for having black bears, and black bears love people food. My dad of course knew this and took precautions to make sure Yogi didn't wake us up while he tore apart our campsite that night. About 1 or 2 AM my dad and mom got woken up by this growling sound. My dad fearing the worst got his magnum and jumped out of the tent to face the bear. There was no bear. There was still a growling sound. He and mom checked everywhere, and then they realized it was louder by the tent. They checked inside and found that I was still asleep and snoring like a growling bear. My dad then gave me the nickname "Bear" for scaring the hell out of him that night on a camping trip.

As I got older relations with my dad became strained. All that my dad ever wanted was to be a police officer, because then he would be a somebody. A man in uniform gets respect. This view point might have simply been what a Freudian would call "youngest child syndrome". I disagree. He just wanted his family to be proud of him and to respect him. In the Italian culture being a man means you provide for your family and you do it well. If you do not do that then you are a dishonor.

It didn't help that many members of his family told him that he could do better; now in the Italian culture when your family says you need to do better they are not offering help, they are shaming you.

When he decided to quit the force and get a new job something changed in him. Be began to only hunt for money not fulfillment. I do want to make one thing clear. My dad's tenacity and penchant for self-sacrifice insured that we never went without. There was always food on the table, and the same roof over our heads, and presents at Christmas. There were times when there wasn't as much or as high of quality, but my dad provided for his family to the best of his ability. For that alone I honor him.

The thing was I was depressed, and so was my dad. Many times during my childhood my dad would go through jobs like party girls go through boyfriends. At this time I had issues with the Church and school, and my dad yelling at me during the summer when I would spend all day inside watching PBS to get off my fat ass and go outside and pull weeds didn't help. You see, depression makes people heavy, and I was no exception. At 11 years old I had man-boobs, moobs, or bitch-tits as they are commonly known. And my dad jumping through job after job wasn't helping. One of his longest lasting positions was working for a soft drink company as a shelf stalker. It was back-breaking labor for minimum wage at best. My dad was always exhausted and therefore cranky, and he tended to take it out on mom and me emotionally. Then one day he fell at work and hurt his neck. Now because it did not happen on company property my dad was at first denied workman's comp. We had to fight to get my dad medical care to prevent him from being paralyzed. He did eventually get treatment and made a full recovery.

Not long after, he quit that job and became a police officer again this time for a different city. It was a new kind of hell for him. His commanders did not like him because of his religion. As I said before my dad is a proud Catholic; the majority of the force was Mormon and very prejudice. They sent him on very dangerous assignments, and tried to get him killed. Sadly, my dad brought that energy home again and again. My mom and I suffered through that for quite some time, and it almost ended the marriage. My dad did finally realize what he was doing and what his great and wonderful job was doing to him and his family and he left the force. He started working at small computer company answering service calls. He was surprisingly happy. He was making good money, and not getting shot at. What's not to like? It was at this time that we got our first computer and—wait for it—the internet. All praise Al Gore, Lord and Creator of the internet! Hallowed be his name!

Just kidding, but seriously that computer as slow and simple as it was, compared to what we have now that is, was a godsend. I took to it like a pig to mud. Thank you daddy, god bless you! I surfed everywhere. I downloaded stuff and caught viruses. I chatted and got bored and confused with the inane things people talk about. I was 11 or 12 years old when my love affair began with certain men's magazine known for its tasteful albeit racy pictures of beautiful women highlighted by the silhouette of a rabbit's head.

One day my dad caught me on the site. When he asked me what I thought I was doing, I replied, "Would you rather I was on a guy-on-guy site?" He tilted his head to the side and said, "Good point." My dad never worried if I was straight no matter how flamboyant I may have been later in life. One of the bad things that came out of me and my fascination with that magazine's website was a porn addiction that plagued me for years and screwed up a lot of my life. I do want to say that I never used the magazine's pictures as my material. I have always considered it art, just like any piece of Botticelli, Michelangelo, or even da Vinci. I used other things. Nothing that was depraved or disgusting or illegal; it was just people having sex. And that is all.

I'm sure you're wondering about my mom. She is just as good as my dad perhaps more. Her stream of revenue for the family was and is much more reliable. My mom has worked my entire life and has only had 4 jobs that I know of and she has never been fired or quit prematurely. She didn't always make that good of money or like what she was doing, but I could always count on her. When I was a baby she was a waitress at a local steak house, and she worked her ass off. Then she worked in retail, and rose to become manager over shoes and apparel. For a year when I was in grade school she worked as a teacher at a middle school teaching developmentally challenged kids. Then almost immediately after that when the store she was working at began to have trouble she got out became a bill collector. Not bad for someone with no education past high school. During the darkest times in my family, my mom has always been our guiding light and our beacon of hope. I love my mother deeply, and if anyone messes with her in any way you do not want to know what I will do to them.

Most of the events around my mom and I are simple day to day stuff. She took me to school when she could. She picked me up when she could. She made me lunches and dinners and other meals that would make a king bow to her in respect. My dad also has this talent, but for the most part only with dinner. It is from both my parents that I get my penchant, my talent, my skill and joy of cooking.

One of the main impacts of my mom on my life is her philosophy with money. She is ultraconservative with it. When you are starving and scraping to get by this is a good thing, but she did not teach me really how to use my money to my advantage when I have it. I have a mental barrier there; it is being broken down however. My mom did teach me a lot about a very special part of my life that I will get to in a completely different section.

One of the things my mom did screw up on me with was when she taught me about dating and women. My mom taught me that good women don't like sex, and that I would have to be really careful when dating, because if I found a girl that liked sex she was probably bad and didn't actually like me at all she was just using me. In my mom's defense, I probably misinterpreted what she said. What she meant was to be careful don't get anyone pregnant and treat my woman like a lady. I thought she meant don't touch them, don't talk to them, just leave them alone. You will see the effect of that in the section about women.

My mom did teach me a very important lesson that has served me very well in my life and has probably kept a pistol out of my mouth on more than one occasion. She taught me to always look at the positive side of life. She taught me that if the glass is half empty and if you take a drink then the glass is now empty. But if the glass is half full then you still have one more drink. This means no matter how bad this world gets, no matter how dark the night we can still get through it if we are not willing to give up.

My mom went through hell before I was born. As a kid she was beaten nearly every day of her life by her father. When she had my sister at 18 so she could qualify for a full ride scholarship to medical school, her family said she couldn't do that because what would the neighbors think. Then they effectively disowned her and forced her to marry a drunk and a drug addict—not my dad, my sister's dad—who was in a lot of ways a replay of her dad. My mom only made minimum wage up until I was about ten. By all accounts she should at least be an alcoholic or addicted to pain killers. She isn't and never was.

My mom and my dad gave me something that is very important. It is encoded in my very DNA. We never give up. We will fight to our last breath. If you tell us we're beaten, we go harder and find new ways. You want to see the American ideal, look at my face and at the faces of the people I come from. We survive at all costs. We may not be rich. We may not have power. We may not be pretty. But we have our pride and we will see another day. And we will rise stronger and better than we were before.

My mom's side of the family reaches all the way back to the New England colonies. The Irish part of my family came over just after the Mayflower. One of my ancestors learned how to fish, gut that fish, eat the fish and use the guts to fertilize corn so it will grow in sand. His decedents were soldiers in the American Revolution.

The German part arrived sometime in the early 19th century. They were fleeing the land wars started by the likes of Napoleon, the Hapsburgs and various German dukes. This part of my family arrived in a place that didn't like them, but they assimilated. Along the Irish, the Germans were part of the "Native Americans" of the Civil War period. They were native because they had been born here.

The Romanian and Italian parts arrived at about the same time in the early 20th century. The Romanians were actually fairly rich. They were an off shoot of the old Romanian royal family. In fact I am related by marriage to Vlad Tepes—the real Dracula, and he was a prince not a count and not a vampire but he did have issues processing iron properly; a trait which many in my family share including me. My family actually cut off his head in battle and retook the throne. Now the Romanians were coming to America because they smelled war brewing in Europe. When you have the genetic memories of a people that have been hunted everywhere they've gone, you tend to notice when things are going to turn bad.

Many people think that because I am Romanian I should like vampires. I do not, and I do not like anything that glorifies them. The reason is because I as a Gypsy find the glorification of vampires obscene. This is why. Gypsies are not European; they are actually from the Asian Steppe from about the Afghanistan/Pakistan area.

About 2000 years ago, there was a big civil war, and the Gypsies lost. They had to find a new place to live. They couldn't head north or east because of the Himalayas, and assuming they survived they would run into the Chinese, and the Chinese didn't like anybody anyway. South was out as an option because that was the home of their enemy. West was the only way that they could go. The Gypsy clans packed up and headed into the Persian Empire.

It went relatively well. They weren't exactly welcome, but they weren't being shot at either. Some clans decided to stay, and they intermingled with the local population. The majority of the Gypsies continued on to the eastern coast of the Mediterranean Sea and Judea. The Byzantine Empire had just been born out of the Eastern Roman Empire. Many of the southern provinces were in a mild state of turmoil due to the Western Roman Empire starting to fall. The Gypsies began to trade and mingle with the local Jewish population. It is here that for the next couple hundred years my people learned how to use divination and fortune telling. They took Jewish mysticism called Kabbalah to a whole new level, and it cemented the bond between Jews and Gypsies that can still be seen to this day.

In about the 4th century the Western Romans had fallen to the constant onslaught of the Germanic hordes, and internal corruption. Politically everything west of the Danube River was up for grabs effectively. The Gypsy clans that arrived at this time saw their chance. They started to settle in what are now Romania and Hungary and Austria. These are the clans from which I come from.

As the villages started to be built for the Gypsies, the newly formed Germanic kingdoms began to consolidate their power and sure up their lands. One day a young Gypsy man was out hunting deer for his family. He found a deer, and killed it. As he was taking it back home he was stopped by a patrol of Germanic soldiers. They told him that he had killed a deer that belonged to the king. The young man apologized, and offered the deer to the soldiers. Not good enough. The soldiers killed the young man and razed his newly built village to the ground. As word spread throughout the Gypsy communities, they went on high alert. In a very short time all the clans were reduced to nomads again. Every time they would try to set down roots the local governing body would come and try to kill them. As a result the nomadic way of life was bred into the Gypsy people.

This made them opportunists, thieves, con-artists and masters of the natural world. It is in my blood to be able to survive when I have nothing. I do not use it very often, but it is there. In about the 15th or 16th century a movement grew in one of the Romanian clans. These Romanian clans had faired a little better than the other clans. They had managed to intermingle with some of the local populace and even become part of the ruling body. This is how Prince Vlad entered my family. Many of the clans were still rather nomadic. They decided that they were tired of running, and they were going to settle down and hold their ground to the last man. They needed land to start with first. So they cooked up a story that was pulled from the local folklore of the Romanians and

Germanic Austrians that lived in the Carpathian Mountains. This story would come to be what we in the modern world call “vampire”. They spread this lie around the Germanic peoples in the hopes that it would scare them away long enough for an actual town or perhaps a city to be built.

It back fired. The Gypsies had not counted on just how zealous Germans can be in their beliefs centering in Christianity. So the Gypsies got invaded…again. They found people like me with teeth longer than average and strong senses and bodies to be used as evidence of the reality of vampires and to maybe scare the Germans away. This just egged the Germans on in their attempt to purify the heathen lands of Romania and kill all the evil that was living there.

As it stands now to the best of my knowledge, all European Gypsies are nomadic; they have given up. Nobody likes them. Nobody wants them around. So they go from city to city and country to country just trying to survive. Genetic diseases are common in the European clans due to inbreeding. My family was able to escape this fate by coming to the States when they did.

I hate all these vampire stories on TV and in books because they are warping something that was a last ditch effort into something of a caricature. Vampires are not wonderful. They are not romantic. They are dangerous. The energy around the idea of them is evil. Please people stop screwing around with it.

The Italians were similar to the Romanians. The Sicilian arm came here because of the growth of the old country Mafia. The mainlanders came here for better work and to send money back to Italy to help out the family. Ironically the ones that stayed in Italy started a company similar to Singer or Schwinn while the ones that came to the States largely stayed rough necks.

As for all of you people out there that think all Italians are Mafia I will say this: no members of my family including myself to the best of my knowledge are members of La Cosa Nostra. That being said, if you think I am I won't argue with you, because if you think I'm a deadly gangster then you'll probably leave me the hell alone.

It was about the time I became a teenager that I stopped being called "Ricky" and started being called "Richard". In the Italian culture you are given a full name at birth like "Michael" or "Jonathan" or "Giovanni". As a kid you are called by a lesser version of that name usually ending with an "ee" sound. Your full name is earned when you gain honor and or prestige within the family and society. This usually happens somewhere in the teens or twenties. It started happening for me when I was about thirteen or fourteen. It started with me and my mom and dad and eventually spread through the family with only a few people not conforming. Now depending on who you are and our relationship will depend on what you call me. Most people call me "Richard"; very few still call me "Ricky"; only my closest friends call me "Dick".

I was horrible as a teenager. I'm actually amazed that my parents didn't sell me, kill me, or have me committed. For the most part I was a good kid. I got straight A's 99 percent of the time. I never snuck out. I never did drugs. If I did do something that I knew was wrong which was a rare occurrence, I always made sure that I wouldn't get caught, and usually I didn't. The problem came with my mood swings. I could go from normal to needing an exorcist in a few minutes. I now know that this was the result of an internal issue caused by malnutrition (teenagers don't eat very well) and stress (my hormones were going crazy and I had 40 hours worth of school plus extra-curriculars plus work). Because of what I and my parents and every family has gone through and is going through when I become a doctor I want to help treat this condition in teenagers and parents. No one is off the hook, both need treatment.

Most of these episodes of emotional instability involved a mild disagreement between me and one or both of my parents most often my mom. I was kind of scared of my dad. Mom would often say something that I would have an opinion about. When I would share it, she would interrupt me. I don't like being interrupted, so I would get mad at her and we would start a yelling match. One morning before school my junior year of high school I was not feeling well. Mom said something to me and I went off on her. Dad came in and tried to break it up. I got fed up and stomped outside. Mom followed me with Dad close behind. I then said something that set my dad off. He pushed my mom out of the way, grabbed me by the back of the hair and pushed me up against the tailgate of his truck. He said in my ear something to the effect of, "You're going to stop this right now. You are going to respect your mother, or are we going to have a problem?" I instantly folded. The fight was over and I lost badly. I spent the rest of the day depressed and shaming myself for what I had done to my mom. I did not eat, which is very typical of me when I'm upset. I was very quiet for about the next week and I refused to make eye contact with anyone.

During my junior year of college tragedy struck my family. I was getting ready for school and something just seemed off. I came down for breakfast and sat next to my dad just like always. Mom was cooking eggs and hash browns while she talked to my niece in Tennessee. She handed the phone to my dad as she handed me my breakfast. As he talked to my niece he started to babble. Then he said, "Sweetheart, can you hold on for a minute?" At that moment a seizure ripped through his body. I grabbed the phone and hung it up. I then grabbed my dad's hands to give him something to focus on. The phone rang again, mom answered. It was my sister wanting to know what was going on. Mom explained everything. She then hung up with my sister and called 911. I checked my dad. He was very disoriented. My mom and dad soon went to the hospital and I was ordered to school. I drove to Sara's house to pick her up as I always did. I was distraught. She was a psych major, and upon seeing me, instantly tried to get the information out of me. I sobbed and told her everything that had happened that morning. She was kind enough to comfort me.

School that day was a near waste. My mind was on my dad only. About half way through the day my mom called me with the news. My dad had actually not had a seizure. As the doctor had put it is was just a reaction to the painkiller that he had been taking for his neck pain. Bullshit! We were missing something. My mom called an old friend of hers from high school who had grown up to be a neurosurgeon. It took my mom at least 5 calls before he called her back. After about a 30 minute conversation he agreed to see my dad. A few days later my dad went in for an MRI and something was found. He had a tumor in his spinal cord the size of a pea with what looked like little tendrils coming off of it. We all sat down and spoke with the doctor. It was indeed cancerous, and the only real option was surgery. Chemo wouldn't work because of the lack of direct blood flow to the area, and radiation would likely kill him anyway.

The procedure was scheduled for about 2 weeks later. In that time my dad aged 20 years. His hair turned white and his movements became very slow. Mom and I shut off almost completely emotionally so we could function with day-to-day life. While we waited for his operation date every member in the family, and I mean every member, started prayer circles for my dad. We had people from many different religions, not just various sects of Christianity. We had Buddhists, Mormons, Catholics, Baptists, Anglicans, Lutherans, Pagans and Gnostics all praying for my dad for at least 2 solid weeks. The day finally came and he went under the knife.

He survived! When my dad was in post-op my mom and I spoke with the doctor for his report. He told us that everything went better than expected and my dad should have a near full recovery. He went on to say that it was a miracle that my dad even made it to the operation. He said that 98 percent die before the operation and 99 percent die on the table. My mom and I decided that the prayers did something, whatever it was. When my dad came out of anesthesia he was checked for mobility and sensory. Mobility was good but sensory was down to about 70 percent. A few days later my dad was released from the hospital and he was sent home to begin recuperation and physical therapy.

For the operation the doctor had to cut from about C3 to C6 and he removed the back sections of the vertebrae to get to the spinal cord. This of course meant that my dad's central nervous system was exposed to the outside world with the exception of some stitches and a calcium based goo that the doctor had put on the vertebrae to help them heal. Still this was a very dangerous condition for my dad to be in, so he was placed in the hands of a home care nurse and physical therapist to speed his recovery. The nurse was great. She was very nice and came around when my dad needed her but she soon realized that my mom and I had everything under control. The physical therapist on the other hand was a different story.

We only saw him 3 times and that was 2 times too many. Let me explain. The first time he met with my dad he did a physical assessment on him and gave my dad some mobility and dexterity exercises to perform so his body would start to re-sequence around some of the damaged neurons from the operation and things went great sensory information started to return. The therapist returned a week later and decided to make my dad do some more intense work like jumping off of a short stool and making him jump up and down. I looked at the back of my dad's head as he was doing this and noticed that he was leaking spinal fluid. That's a very bad thing. My mom ordered the therapist and my dad to stop.

"Why?" the therapist asked.

"He's leaking spinal fluid," my mom replied.

"Spinal fluid? Why is he leaking spinal fluid?"

"He had spinal surgery a few weeks ago. The wound hasn't closed yet," I said.

"Oh oops, sorry."

The therapist left and came back a week later after my mom had spoken with the doctor and was assured that everything would be fine. On the third visit the therapist did the exact same thing of making my dad jump up and down and then trying to lift 5 pound weights. Again he started to leak spinal fluid. My mom tended to my dad while I took care of the therapist. I was going to kill him. As I began to dress him down he acted as though he had no knowledge of my dad's condition. This only fueled my anger. My mom did manage to quiet me down before I did something that I would have regretted, and the therapist was banished from our house. She ran my dad up to the hospital to have his neck repaired while I calmed down.

Over about the next year my dad slowly got better. He would spasm every so often due to the damage in his spinal cord. Every few months he would go in for an MRI to verify that the cancer had indeed been eradicated. To this day my dad is alive and well with the minor exceptions of occasional tremors and decreased physical sensation. He has been cancer free since the operation and remains so to this day.

For some reason my old man has always had a thing with getting sick. After the cancer episode a couple of years later he contracted staph. This is a fairly deadly bacterium that naturally lives on our skin and kills other things that come too close like staph from other people. It turns deadly when it gets inside the body and starts to spread. It was everywhere in my dad. The doctors put him on some adaptive antiseptic drug that was pumped directly into his veins, but it was only stemming the tide. Then my mom read about an herb that nearly everyone has at the ready—oregano. Specifically the oil of oregano; it is one of the only things that will kill staph. So in addition to the doctor's treatments my dad started taking the oil, and so did Mom and I. It tastes horrible. Oil of oregano is one of the foulest things that I have ever taken. It burns all the way down. You cry, you cough, and then you smell like a sandwich. However, it got the job done. Within about a week to two weeks my dad was free of infection, and neither of us showed signs of contamination. Afterward we took some probiotics to rebuild the bacteria in our bodies that the oregano had killed. After the episode with the staph my Italian cousin that I spoke about earlier told my dad that he needed a new hobby.

My dad and I have done some remodeling projects together. They were actually kind of fun. We re-landscaped the front yard the year after his cancer surgery. We did the upstairs bathroom right before he came done with the staph; I think I might know the cause. Then we did the kitchen. I assisted my dad and served as a second pair of eyes and another brain for when he started to get tired. My mom had me do this because she knew that my dad would listen to me more than he would listen to her.

The remainder of things involving my parents and family will be handled in the final section.

FRIENDS AND THE "DAYS OF THUNDER"

I have a lot of friends. People just seem to like me, which is something that I just don't understand sometimes. I don't consider myself to be that great of a person. I grew up believing that because of the way people around me acted that friendship was a commodity. It could be bought and sold readily. I will explain.

As a kid my world was really small. In the 1980's and early 1990's the world wasn't exactly safe. I didn't go outside very often, except for when Mom was with me. The reason for this was most of the people that lived in my neighborhood were 30 years or older. Yes there were families, but with all the racial and religious prejudice that existed we really didn't have friends in the community. Until a family from Jackson Hole moved in across the street. They had 2 boys, the younger being 4 years older than me. I was 4 years old and very excited that I could actually have a friend and not just a bunch of kids that I didn't really know. So our parents introduced us and we hit it off. M. J. and I were really good friends; the summer before I started kindergarten we were nearly inseparable. We played in the dirt. We played this weird thing that came from this movie that he just loved about a guy that could move things by thinking about it and he carried a sword made out of light. I didn't get it, but I played anyway. M. J. was my closest and bestest friend until he got too old to hang out with me anymore when I was about eight or nine.

In the fall of 1989 I started school for the first time. My mom told me to make a bunch of new friends and have fun and learn a lot. I was so excited that I actually peed myself. Nobody cared though. I made a bunch of new friends in about a month. There was T. L., M. C., and a kid named Zach who was a little weird but as a kid weird is good. T. L. had a bunch of toys and his mom and dad were nice they reminded me of my own parents. T. L. and I got along great. I would go over to his house he would come over to mine, and we would tear the place up like pint-sized rock stars. Then one day at school M. C. decided he wanted to be my friend more than he was. M. C. and I both went to the same church, T. L. wasn't a member. M. C. pointed out that I was more like him than I was T. L. and we should play. Whatever, I'm easy.

My dad and I had built a club house for me and my friends to play in right before I started kindergarten. When I did have kids come over I was the cool kid because I had a big backyard with a clubhouse on stilts and a slide. Back then my parties, especially my birthday parties were off the hook. The guest list was huge and everybody always had a good time. T. L. and his main group of friends would come over and mix with my main group of friends, and we would have a time bigger than what are often seen at most Hollywood royalty parties.

Then one day in the first grade I was hanging out with M. C. in my club house and we were just talking. He said that he had something he wanted to try with me. I thought it was some new game he had thought up. So I closed my eyes like he said and waited. I don't entirely know what I was expecting, but what he did surprised me. I felt him grab my hand and then I felt a soft slightly wet pressure on my cheek. My eyes jumped open to see M. C. attempting to cuddle with me. He had kissed me on the cheek, and was apparently falling in love with me. I kicked him out and never hung out with him again. A few months later his family moved to Orem and I never saw him again. When I finally told my dad about what had happened his jaw hit the floor.

He tried to explain to me what a "gay" was. I didn't get it. I was a kid; I just thought he was weird. In retrospect all the warning signs were there, and they were all the stereotypical ones. At the risk of insulting the homosexual community and probably anyone else, I want to go on record of saying this: I am friends now with many members of the gay community. While homosexually is unappealing to me from a carnal point, I will fight for the right of all people to live as they wish in whatever way they wish and to enjoy everything that anybody and everybody does. To men that are gay: I am your friend, but if you hit on me and do not get that I am in fact straight and continue to pester me we will have a problem. Otherwise, feel free to eat at my table.

After M. C. left I started hanging out with M. J. more again. There was another kid on the street that was just as cool named C. L. The three of us were always up to something and getting into trouble which was usually C. L.'s idea. He was kind of troubled. Right about when I started Cub Scouts, C. L.'s dad got transferred to Las Vegas. He of course moved, but returned a few years later very different and very scary. We were no longer friends. I did get to see him the summer before I moved to LA. He had finally made peace with his demons. He was living a good normal life with a very beautiful wife.

I started Cub Scouts through the Church and had a great time. During the summers we would go up one of the canyons near Salt Lake City called Millcreek to some day camps for crafts, activities, get out of our parents' hair and throw some money away at the camp trading post. Loved it. Had a blast. During this time I made a lot of new friends that I went to school and had church with but never really hung out with. One kid I met through Scouts, D. K. came over to my house for the first time to play, and we had a really good time. After he left my dad tried to open the closet to grab his coat for work and the handle came off the door. I of course got yelled at for it, but I didn't do it. D. K. had palmed a screwdriver and in the course of our games he had gone around my house and at least loosened all the screws that he could. My dad wasn't happy. D. K. never came over again, but I did go over to his house. That was a very strange place. His family was huge. He was the third oldest of twelve. Even by Mormon standards this family was massive. The place was always dirty and always loud. I started to understand why D. K. was the way that he was.

As my career in Scouts progressed I was re-united with my old friend B. S. He had changed in the 8 or 9 years since we had hung out in the nursery at church. He had become reclusive and nerdy, but he was still my friend. I did what I could to hang out with him, and we did every so often. But because of the social stigma around my dad being Catholic and I being his unbaptized and therefore Hell-bound son, I did not hang out with anyone outside of scouts, school, and church stuff.

Because of the intermittent nature of my friendships during my childhood and preteen years I missed out on a lot of stuff. I didn't play massive games of hide-and-seek in my neighborhood. I didn't go on long bike rides through the town with my friends and try to find Curly's gold. I never had a crush on the girl next door that climaxed with an innocent kiss in a boat on family vacation, etc. What many people call a "childhood", I didn't have. I went from being a kid of 8 to a teenager in 2 years, and starting puberty at 9 didn't help.

As a kid for the most part I was a freak. From 8 to 13 years of age are some of the worst years of my life for many reasons. I didn't have a best friend or even a good friend to turn to during the darkest times when my dad was out of work and my mom was working 2 or 3 jobs to keep us from going under. My sister's boyfriend was the closest thing I had to a brother at the time and he would mess with me the way a brother should, but I didn't understand that so it made things worse. At school I was treated like an animal, so guess what I became.

You see, starting puberty so early and in a community where if you are different means you are evil, takes its toll on a boy's sanity. Because I was sprouting hair everywhere and my voice was changing and I was having very primal urges, I figured I was turning into a werewolf.

Don't act surprised! For God sakes I was 9 and alone. This started in the fourth grade, so I went to the library to figure out what was going on with me, B. S.

came along. I got some books on werewolves, mostly the myth of them and decided that's what I was becoming. Had I someone to talk to about what I was going through—that is starting the process of becoming a man—I never would have had the horrible life that I did as a kid. But left to my own idiotic devices lycanthropy was the only "logical" conclusion.

So in fourth grade I played to it as a strength. My classmates loved it, I was cool! I still don't know why, but I was. I didn't really get together with anyone, but school was bearable. I came back with it during my fifth grade year and played it up even more. It did not work, instead of being praised I was reviled and it made my depression worse. I became extremely self-destructive and very mean especially to animals. While I never killed any I was abusive mostly to my cat, Daniel who we got as a kitten when I was five. He was my only true friend, and I repaid his innocent kindness with fear and pain. To this day I have remorse for those actions. He and I have made peace; thank God I did it before he died when I was 22.

When my parents saw what I was becoming, they sent me to a child psychiatrist. Waste of time, waste of money. He gave me a bunch of little sayings to boost my self-esteem, and I told him what he wanted to hear. That kept me off meds and out of the hospital. However I was still sick and very scary. Very few people wanted to be around me and I played to that. At least they weren't hurting me directly. So by the sixth grade I had turned completely reclusive and very anti-social. I tried to change, but the damage had been done. The only way out of this social and mental tailspin was to completely get away from everyone that I had gone to grade school with and start somewhere new. We couldn't move, but I could go to another middle school. So I elected to attend a different middle school from the majority of my class and re-invent myself.

I do want to say this to any parent of any boy reading this: when he starts puberty if he hasn't started already please have "the talk" with him. Do not under any circumstances let the school system do it for you. The information tends to be biased to sex is evil and everyone has a disease and the information is given far too late to be useful. Tell your son that everything is normal, and he can talk to you about anything. Then when he comes to you no matter how tired or angry at the world you are please hear him and help him. If you can do this you will prevent any form of lycanthropy and or vampirism from rising up and taking hold. So please educate yourself on the human body especially sexual stuff and inter-gender interaction. Keep it scientific and do not use the clergy of any religion; they tend to mess with your head, I think I would know. So please don't just concentrate on your girls, take care of your boys too.

Upon entering Mt. Jordan Middle School I had only one friend, B. S. We went to orientation together and we carpooled. The thing was his mom insisted on joining us. I thought it was lame, but I guess 2 geniuses are just too dumb to figure out how the school is laid out. B. S. and his mom soon became my ride to and from school due to my mom's work hours. At school I started making a lot of new friends, but I started to notice the exact same cultural differences that existed between me and the kids at Edgemont. So I decided that I needed to change, and I changed my thought processes to reflect those of the majority of the students. This worked well and people started to like me or at least hate me less.

I remember the first day of school in homeroom. I was placed in the back due to my name starting with V. I guess it's the fairest way to set a seating chart, because kids are just too stupid to figure out that not only do you sit in a chair, but in the same chair so the teacher can figure out who you are by your location instead of your face. There was this kid sitting directly in front of me two rows up. He was lanky and kind of ugly with oddly accentuated facial features: big nose, big eyes, big ears, and a big mouth. He turned around and looked at me, I saw fear in his eyes probably because I already had facial hair—I started shaving that Christmas. That kid was S. G. and he became very important to me in the next few years. I will leave it there for now.

As the weeks progressed I met a bunch of new people as I said before. I met a set of twins that I didn't realize were twins. I had a class with one and lunch with the other; I thought the other was the one I had class with. That was embarrassing. I met B. G., C. A., Vairin and a kid named Bum who to this day I still don't understand the origin of that name. There were so many people that I met and felt welcomed by that I don't really want to talk about because it would bore you. That being said my social life didn't change much from how it was during grade school. I hung out with B. S., but very sparingly. That is until the near end of the year when I met Scott.

He was overweight, quiet, isolated and a little suspicious of everyone. We had first period English together, but I had never spoken to him until the teacher set us together to work on a small journalism project for our end of the year project. It took a little while, but Scott did eventually open up. Over the summer we became very close friends. We hung out a lot. We shared secrets like how bad our childhoods were and what girls we liked. There have been very few people in this world that I have had that kind of connection with, especially at thirteen. We were best friends by the start of eighth grade. Scott had not only replaced B. S. in my life, but outperformed him as a human being. Getting B. S. to hang out was like pulling teeth, and I always had to call him. Scott would call me.

As our friendship deepened, I began to meet more and more of Scott's friends. My circle of friends grew as a result. There was always somebody new hanging around, especially girls. They weren't the best looking lot, but girls are girls when you're thirteen. It was at this time that I met A. W. and S. B. The former of these two girls was gorgeous and Scott's main love interest. She was blonde and slim and kind of fun. Scott had been in love with her since grade school and she didn't know. I really wanted to help him out, so I started to set things up for my friend for him to tell her how he felt. He however always chickened out. S. B. was A. W.'s best friend, and I'm sorry to say this, very unattractive. She looked just like A. W. with the exception of having massive teeth and gums. S. B. and I did not really get along and in many ways we still don't.

For some reason, the longer I knew Scott the more friends he had. When I met him he had very few friends, then all of the sudden he became magnetic. All social gatherings revolved around Scott and his house. We had friendly poker nights, video game days and big parties with everyone. One event involved Scott, me and this redheaded girl that I won't name. We were in Scott's basement playing a first-person-shooter video game. In a first-person-shooter you are a person holding a gun in the game and you walk around and blow stuff up. We took turns and had a blast no pun intended. My turn came up so Scott and the girl decided to go upstairs to get something to drink while I played. I died fairly quickly in about 5 minutes. I went upstairs to see what my friends were up to. As I got to the landing I heard this conversation:

Girl: "Wow, it's big."

Scott: "Thank you I've had a lot of fun with it."

Girl: "You said it was big, but you didn't say it was this big. It just keeps going and going. Hey what's that thing up there in the corner?"

Suspecting the worst I burst into the dining room to see Scott and the girl fully clothed and standing there innocently.

"What are you two doing?" I asked suspiciously.

"Just looking at the backyard," Scott replied. "What did you think we were doing?"

"Nothing. Never mind."

Scott's house was a ranch style. The backyard was huge, and it had this little clubhouse way in the back corner that had been built for reasons similar to my own clubhouse. However, because it was at ground level and poorly ventilated we never used it. And it being infested with various species of vermin and with biting and stinging insects and spiders I'm sure didn't mean anything either. Living in this back yard was Scott's dog, Piper. She was a young Scottish border collie. She had a black back, white belly, and white paws. She was sweet as could be, and she loved to give hugs by jumping up and wrapping her forelegs around your waist and leaning in. She was treated very well, and got to come in the house all the time. I miss that dog.

Now as I said we had friendly poker nights at Scott's place at least once a month. They were friendly for two reasons: first we were teenagers and didn't exactly have money to gamble with; second we were all Mormon and gambling is a sin, we were taking enough of a risk with the face cards as it was. Yeah I know...what do face cards have to do with risk? I don't have a straight answer for that. Near as I can figure they can steal your soul or something dumb like that.

The poker nights themselves were a very ritualized event. I always dealt first. The game was always 5 card draw jacks or better to open with deuces wild. Always a good time. We would start playing no earlier than 8 PM and it was not unheard of for us to continue playing until 3 AM. We played tournament style. When a player was defeated all of his chips were absorbed by the player who won the hand and the antae doubled. For the most part it was always 5 card draw with at least one wild. If you cheated you got thrown off the back deck of the house; it was only used once and not until we were in high school. It was through these poker nights that I became friends with Vairin and B. G.

The girls didn't play poker, but that was beside the point. Scott's parents wouldn't allow any girls over to the house after 9 PM. Not a problem we had plenty of guy friends to fill the other 2 seats so the game had a minimum of 4 players to start. B. G. was the first to join us and stay. I had met him earlier at school, but he was nothing more than somebody to chew the fat with as we waited for the bell to end lunch. Now I got to know him, he was pretty cool. He lived in Japan on a US military base with his dad before moving back to the States. He was short, blonde and heavily built. And could he turn a phrase. B. G. was a laugh a minute except for when he was depressed due to his home situation which sucked. I won't go into it, but suffice to say the place was crowded. Scott and I became his out.

The three of us were inseparable. One day during the spring of our eighth grade year the three of us went to the dollar theater for a movie. In the same strip mall was a nickel arcade, so after the show we decided to go play some games. A miracle occurred as we were checking games. I found a fighting game that used swords, and someone had set it to "free". The three of us took turns on that game all afternoon. We arrived at about one and finally left at five because we were hungry. I was the undisputed champ of the game, because my 2 friends couldn't take me down at all. Boy did our fingers hurt. Another time we went out for some pizza at this chain place by my house. We bought a supreme and dove in. Then Scott found a hair and we ate for free. It soon became a regular thing for us to go out and Scott to find something wrong with the food and us eating for free. It was legendary.

That summer Scott and I decided to perform a classic TV show episode about a comedian's life in New York with some of our friends. We were going to record it and have in on file for our professional portfolios for when we were older. There was a problem, we didn't have the script and I was heading to Nashville for a wedding between the mother of my brother-in-law and her boyfriend. I was 14 and couldn't get out of it. We decided that we would begin shooting when I got back 2 weeks later.

The following is a record of what I have been told. I actually have no memory of events with a few small exceptions near the beginning of the trip.

We, and when I say "we" I mean Mom, decided that we should drive from Salt Lake City, Utah to Nashville, Tennessee. It would take us a couple of days to make the 1700ish mile trip, but my parents wanted me to see Graceland and actual prairie farms and to see what it was like to see and actual river like the Mississippi. So in the middle of June Mom, Dad and I all piled into my mom's tiny Mitsubishi Mirage Coupe and set out for the South.

I could hear the banjo music playing before we made it to Wyoming, mostly because my parents only listened to country and the only cassettes my mom wanted to bring were very old country by Don Williams a brother of the original Hank Williams. Those three cassettes were all we listened to for 1700 miles. I'm sure you want to know, why we didn't bother to check the radio stations for other music even if it was nothing other than country. According to my mom that is against the rules of a road trip along with using air conditioning because it wastes gas, or rolling down the windows because then other people will think that we're too poor to afford air conditioning. As a result of this mind numbing monotony of entertainment that is inherent in a road trip, and given that my parents aren't the talkative sort I chose to sleep for most of the trip. My dad woke me up when something interesting came up like a big river or a big city or food.

We drove pretty much straight through to North Platte, Nebraska with the minor exceptions of gas and various biological functions. We decided to stop in North Platte for the night. I thought it was actually kind of nice. I could smell the corn fields and the cows very well, and I actually enjoyed it. It felt like home in a really weird way. We found a tavern where we could get some food. We went in and were sat by our waitress, who I thought was kind of hot. We ordered, and we learned something.

In Utah chicken fried steak is a large chicken breast that has been fried in lard. Everywhere else on the planet apparently it is a beef steak fried in chicken fat. Yeah I know...Utah is weird. This is significant because my mom has an odd allergy to beef that no doctor has been able to figure out. If she eats even a small amount of that glorious meat her intestines twist in knot and she loses a lot of blood very quickly. So why the hell did my mom do something so stupid as to willingly eat poison? We didn't know that chicken fried steak was beef. Before we had even made it to Tennessee my mom nearly died. Thanks to my dad's paramedic training she was saved from a trip to the hospital and a pine box. We got up the next morning and set out for Memphis. We arrived the next day, because my mom wanted to see some tourist trap that I don't remember and I don't want to remember.

We pulled into Memphis the following morning and started toward Graceland. We learned something else. The palace of The King of Rock-n-Roll is located in the bad part of town. We were not only the only white people for miles, but the only people with money for miles. Now because of this we made the assumption that we were in a lot of trouble because in the 90's racism was still around in the South, just nobody talked about it. We rolled by a bunch of people and they looked at us like, "What the hell are you people doing here?" I'm not sure if it was the fact that our plates were from Utah or because we were honkies, but my fourteen-year-old head was going crazy.

We found Graceland, parked, and entered the museum. I thought it was a little interesting. Clearly there were color schemes that could not be found in nature, and design ideas that made no sense especially to a sheltered boy such as me. We got to Elvis's grave and saw the old women who were weeping over is final resting place even though he had been dead for twenty-some-odd years then. I didn't get it, but I didn't get a lot of stuff back then. Mom and Dad were having a great time, I however was not. School had taught me not to drink water; I'll get into why later. The day that we were in Memphis was unseasonably hot and extremely humid. I had come from a very dry place, and was now in a very wet place. No one had told me to drink a lot of water when it is really hot and really humid. The atmosphere was so overbearing on me that I could only go a few feet before I had to sit down. It was so humid that I felt like I was swimming across the street. I almost passed out several times, and I probably had mild heat stroke. So kids, please drink water.

So from Graceland we set out for a town near Nashville called Franklin to meet up with my sister, her husband and his mother. We had a few days to kill before the wedding, so we did some stuff that amounted to a regular vacation. I don't actually remember any of it. We went to Lynchburg to see the Jack Daniels Distillery or the "Tennessee Temple" as my dad called it. We went to the Grand Ole Opery, and I have stood on the stage or so I'm told. We went to Loretta Lynn's Mansion and hung out by the river that runs near her place. My dad was unfortunate enough to catch a parasite there called chiggers. Chiggers are a mite that is kind of a cross between a flea and a tick. They burrow into the skin, drink your blood and lay their eggs in the fresh wound that they made. The result is horrible, maddening itching and secondary infections. Chiggers are caught by walking on the grass where their little colony lives and they jump onto your bare legs. The only way I know of to kill them is by coating the affected area with clear nail polish and suffocating the parasite. My poor dad caught chiggers pretty bad. His legs were covered in red spots almost like measles and he could not stop scratching. So we did the coating and everything was fine about an hour later.

The day before the wedding we went to a plantation museum called the Hermitage. This was the home President Andrew Jackson. He was president during the 1830's and has his image on the $20 bill. My mom believed at the time that not only was he the hero of the Battle of New Orleans but he was given the nickname “Stonewall” for his work during the American Civil War in the 1860’s. No. These are 2 completely different people please get them straight. At the Hermitage I was introduced to a lot of Antebellum Southern culture that had been preserved at this plantation; including something that I will get to later due to the strange nature of the experience.

The next day was the wedding and it went well. After the festivities the following day, Mom, Dad and I packed up and left for Utah. We went by way of St. Lewis where we stopped for lunch at a diner with the theme of the Spirit of St. Lewis. I managed to scare our waitress there by accidentally sneaking up on her. I felt kind of bad. About 2 days and several tornado dodges later, the three of us rolled into Salt Lake City at about 4 AM. We were spent. Our nerves were frayed. I told my mom that I will never do a cross country road trip like that again. I was wrong. The following year we drove to Seattle, had a great time and almost moved there.

Later that day I woke up to a breaking live news report from downtown Salt Lake. A weak F1 tornado had touched down was damaging the façade of the then Delta Center. You see, Utah doesn’t get tornados. This was pretty big news. I was totally amazed. We had been chased by twisters the whole way home; I guessed they just followed us. I called my friend Scott and we got together the following day.

This is the sequence of events as I have been told. I have no other source than my friend Scott.

I biked down to Scott’s place and we grabbed some lunch and then started a movie. We quickly got bored so we went dirt biking in the field behind his neighborhood. We came back to his house, grabbed some water and a snack, finished the movie mostly out of principle, and then I made a suggestion. The South Towne mall was just over State Street, a place I really enjoyed mostly because I was an idiot and I was hoping that I might meet someone there someday. So I talked Scott into biking over with me. We had done it many times, and it was becoming almost as ritualized as our poker nights.

We got down to the light at the intersection of State St. and 10200 S. which was the gateway to the South Towne shopping complex. The light to cross State was green, but the crossing signal was red. I had gotten into the habit recently of going with car traffic instead of pedestrian traffic. I figured that because I legally had the right of way people would just give it to me. In Utah that is an incorrect assumption. If a person is in the road they are culturally considered fair game, and if they happen to be in the way of a car their life is now forfeit. This is how I learned that lesson. I told Scott that we could make it and I started across the street. Scott started to go after me, but he heard a voice in the back of his head scream out "DON'T!" so he stopped. I got halfway across the street and the light changed to yellow. I stopped at the island to wait; this old man in a car in the left turn lane waved me through so I went. I made it to the right turn lane pumping my bike hard, when suddenly a car came up into that turn lane and hit me.

My bike bounced off and I went forward across the car. My head went through the windshield and my right knee went through the driver's window. I bounced off the car and flew about twenty feet then I landed and rolled for about another five. The light changed again and Scott was able to cross; he had never moved so fast in his life. He got to my side; I was unconscious and cut up pretty bad. I came to a few seconds later to the sound of a siren arriving and people touching me and asking me questions that I didn't understand. Scott stayed with me as much as he could. When I was finally loaded into the ambulance, Scott came over to me and asked if I was ok. I said to him, "Scott is the really happening, or are you going to turn into a beautiful woman and kiss me?"

He smiled and said very calmly, "This is really happening man. I will see you at the hospital."

I replied, "OK," and then I smiled.

Then two doors closed to the back of the ambulance and we were off. I woke up again at the hospital just as my mom arrived. I said, "Hey Mom, I made it!" There was this guy though standing beside her and holding her in his arms; I didn't know who his was. He talked to me like he knew me, but I couldn't understand him. I was brought into the ICU and stripped down. I was in a lot of pain and it was apparently all over my body because I punched a nurse in the face when she tried to run an IV. I was swearing at everybody, mostly in Italian. My parents were largely unphased by this, but poor Scott was completely flabbergasted.

When I finally calmed down I looked at him and said, "I'm sorry man, I completely screwed up your day." I passed out again and woke up a couple hours later my mom, dad, sister, brother-in-law, and niece standing at my bedside. My mom was still the only one that I recognized; everyone else had to tell me who they were. I asked where the kid that had been freaked out by what had happened to me had gone. My mom told me he had gone home for the night. My memory was lapsing heavily, and I actually didn't know why I was there or where there was. After they told me about 3 times what had happened a scan was ordered, and I was placed in a very loud tube. I did not like that at all. I was given a sedative so I would hold still. The scan revealed that other than some muscle and tendon damage and some sub-dermal bruising I was fine. I had broken no bones. Aside from being over stimulated my brain was fine. My parents were assured that my memory lapses were in tune with a class 3 concussion (fairly high level), and if they persisted for more than about a week I should come back in for further testing and possibly therapy. I was sent home that night.

The next day Scott came over with a bunch of his video games for me so I could regain some cognitive control. I didn't entirely recognize him, but I knew that he must have been a friend. I was relegated to the couch, where I slept largely upright with my neck in a soft brace. After a few days my memory and various motor skills began to return. I started to play the video games; I didn't do very well, but that wasn't the point and I kind of realized that.

I remember having a horrible stagnant sensation in my neck that in the past I would relieve by popping it. So I popped my neck. Really bad idea. To this day I have several pre-arthritic vertebrae in my neck which will likely fuse when I'm in my forties or fifties. When I was finally able to walk steadily, I remember getting up to use the bathroom and looking in the mirror. I looked like hell. I had a big white neck brace on, 2 black eyes, a swollen lip and severe road rash all down my back not to mention yellow bruising sporadically throughout my body. I was alive however and in largely one piece.

Then my parents started getting weird phone calls from some insurance company and the police. It seems that I had gotten a ticket for blocking an intersection and therefore the insurance wasn't going to cover my injuries even though I was the one that was hit by a car. You see a pedestrian such as a person on a bike, has the right of way in the street regardless of circumstances. That is the federal traffic law and it is upheld by all states. But culturally in Utah if a pedestrian is in the car's way then their life is now forfeit. I have seen and heard a lot of evidence of this in people saying, "Ten points if you hit the guy on the bike." Or in the case of a stray cat or dog, "SWIRVE TO HIT!"

My dad managed to get the charges dismissed on me, but we still had to deal with the insurance. We got a lawyer who wanted to make the woman that hit me pay. We met with the lawyer after a couple of weeks of phone calls. When we sat down she said, "You're not going to like this. All I could do was get Richard's medical bills covered; I couldn't get any restitution money."

I said, "That's okay. That's all I wanted. I don't want her to suffer. She made a mistake, now she is paying for that mistake. Let that be enough."

My lawyer was stunned.

After the ordeal of the accident had been resolved and my intelligence had largely been restored, school started and I got to see my friends again. Scott had told just about everybody what had happened and they were all very glad to see me. They had heard the basics about what had happened to me, and they were amazed that I was still alive.

It was at this time that I began to call this part of my life “the days of thunder”. This is of course a rip from a movie and a country song. The song is actually the inspiration thanks to the line, “How did we ever make it through that?” Near misses happened a lot for us as you will see. Nobody ever really understood what I meant until about the time I started writing this book, but that doesn’t change what high school was for us.

Due to time constraints involving school and the bad omen posed by the accident, Scott and I decided not to go forward with the TV episode remake. We instead focused on our school work and on the regular teenage stuff of friendly poker nights and fantasizing about girls. It at about this time that I learned Scott had an odd obsession with a movie about 4 guys that use advanced physics to capture ghosts. He had both movies memorized along with several episodes of the cartoon. He even had several boxes of the toys in storage somewhere in his room, which was a disaster area. It eventually got so bad that Scott had to sleep in the basement living room. It was because of this mess that he and I came up with the grading scale of a dirty room.

It is based on the degree of devastation that various cities have endured throughout history. Each of the levels is named for one of those cities. The first and cleanest level is Zion: everything is great in its proper place and locatable. The next is Watts: not too bad, if we take the day we can have the place fixed up no problem; at this level there is just a few dirty clothes maybe some papers or books lying around and the bed is unmade. The next is Hamburg: there is a significant mess, help is advisable but not necessarily needed everything is still technically locatable, but the room is messy. The next level is Nagasaki: this is now a room only in the sense that something like sleep happens here; there are dirty clothes not just on the floor but nearly everywhere and finding anything will take time; clean up will require help, but the room is not lost. The worst attainable for living conditions is Har Megiddo (Armageddon): the room is verging on not being livable; it is almost the exact opposite of Zion with a few key differences like no mice are living there, and a regular person will still enter the room although they may not stay long; at this point it is better to just back a large dumpster up to the window and start chucking. The final and most extreme level is Ragnarok, so named because no city can adequately describe the level of filth in a room at this level: it is so bad at this level that the only reasonable recourse is to condemn and quarantine the room/building and move; it has likely been infested with not only bugs but rodents and various other animals as well. Scott's room usually hovered around the Hamburg or Nagasaki levels and only went as far as the Har Megiddo level once or twice that I can remember.

It was during our ninth grade year that the group of friends that I had really started to take on a more stable shape. This was a result of a series of plays that we did in drama club. Everybody that I have mentioned that I met after I started seventh grade except for B. G., C. A. and Bum took part in the plays. We did 2 main plays: the first was *WordRumble* and the second was *Diary of Anne Frank. WordRumble* was written by our drama teacher and pulled from *Romeo and Juliet* and the *Odyssey*. It was poorly written and directed, but for an audience of eighth and ninth graders it wasn't too bad. I played the analog of Odysseus in the play. In *Diary of Anne Frank* I played Mr. Dussel, and I had a great time with it. Scott and I grew closer. Vairin and I became friends. We each made more friends, and I even got a girlfriend out of the deal; more about her later. Our group of friends was one of the best ensembles the school had ever seen and for a period of about 3 or 4 years we were legends.

That winter, Scott, B. G. and I decided to spend New Year's together. It was just the three of us so we decided that just a nice simple party would be just fine. I brought some shrimp, and my game of Risk. B. G. brought some steaks. Scott supplied the house and the sparkling cider. We were all set to have a great time. I managed to bum a ride from dad; I packed up my shrimp, my pillow, and my game and headed down the stairs. I did not notice that I was nowhere near the bottom and I stepped off what I thought was the last stair and ruptured all 3 ligaments on the outside of my right ankle. I was effectively crippled by the sprain. My brother-in-law and dad saw and heard it happen. Being that they had both played football, they had each seen this kind of injury many times. So their advice was, "Walk it off." I couldn't even stand, but I had somewhere to be so I hobbled out into the subfreezing world and to my dad's truck. Oh my god was I in pain, but I was taught that men did not show weakness of any kind and that included physical pain.

I arrived at Scott's a few minutes later and I hobbled to the door. Scott let me in and asked what had happened. I told him. He seemed shocked and asked if I needed any painkiller. I declined. The reason being for some strange reason anything short of an opium derivative has little to no effect on me, so I just don't keep any Tylenol, Ibuprofen, or Advil anywhere where I live. It would just be a waste of money. B. G. arrived and we played our first round of Risk and had dinner. We had a great time. Midnight rolled around and we opened the Martinelli's. B. G. did the honors. At first the bubbles were delayed, and then they flowed out of the bottle and on to the carpet. It was the creation of an inside joke that lasted in the stories of our group for years.

I was in so much pain that night that I had to sleep sitting up to avoid irritating my ankle. I didn't exactly sleep much and had a really bad morning after. I went home after my mom picked me up, and she took care of me. I hobbled on that foot for about 3 weeks and I couldn't properly run on it for an additional month. That was embarrassing. That ankle remained tricky until I entered massage school in 2006 and finally had it corrected.

It was during this hobbled time that some really fun stuff happened. B. G. and I got to host the school talent show. We decided to do it SNL style, complete with fake news. I compiled a top ten list of things that students were writing on the board during detention. None of them were true, but they were funny. They were things like: asbestos is not a preservative, I will not waste chalk, I will not yell fire in a crowded theater, etc. B. G. pretended to be kind of stupid and did a report similar to the famous Gilda Radnor bit of "I love violence (violets)". We had another bit about B. G. that the people loved. It went like this:

Me: The Mount Jordan Drama Club has received many complaints that the actor B. G. is not in enough sketches, skits or plays. The drama club had this to say, "Who's B. G.?"

It was a killer. We had to wait for about 2 minutes for people to stop laughing. We even made some teachers cry from laughter. B. G. had the idea to take some report that I don't remember anymore and read the paper upside down so it came out like gibberish. I then turned it around for him and he continued. As a result of this talent show, B. G. and I were comedic gods in the school.

B. G., Scott, and I had English together that year, and we were assigned to do a dating show project for Penelope from the Odyssey. Being that we were 15 and horny idiots, we of course made this as dirty as we legally could. It was so bad that we almost got suspended, but B. G. stepped up and saved Scott and me. He claimed full responsibility, and begged the teacher to just fail him and give us the minimum grade allowable. B. G. failed the project and had to do extra work, but Scott and I were able to pass with a C or a B. B. G. put himself on the line for us, and it paid off. He became our friend for life. From that day forward I always had his back and he always had mine.

During that year my group of misfit friends came under attack from a rival group of preppy jocks. The 2 female leaders of the group hated us, especially me, B. G., and Scott. So these 2 girls got together one night and wrote a manifesto about how much they hated us and how much they wanted us to die. With me and a few other people in the group they went into very descriptive detail about how they themselves would do it. I was not permitted to read the document, none of us were. We were questioned to see if we had planted it in the locker of one of the girls. Considering none of us knew was exactly was written on the paper, how could we have planted it? This happened not long after the Columbine Massacre, and the school had instituted a very strict no tolerance policy. The 2 girls were expelled, and were not seen by any of us until we went to the high school the following school year.

This attack caused a civil war in the school. My group of friends was under attack for being attacked and defending ourselves. We were called every name in the middle school dictionary of bad names and there were even insinuations that every single one of us was homosexual. In Utah that is really bad, I'm sure you can figure out why. None of it was true, but the school had been torn apart by the incident. We all lost a lot of friends from other groups and we all became very mistrusting of outside people. Our group did not grow for several months until Scott put forth some effort and started bringing new people in again.

It was also during this time that a new kid entered into our group. His name was W. R. He and his family had moved to our little corner of Salt Lake from Helena, Montana. He was and still is a super-nerd. I'm not just talking about the kind of nerds from that show on TV with the hot blonde, no no. I'm talking ugly, greasy, and messy on top of everything you normally think of when you think nerd. So why did we let him hang out with us if he was so repulsive? Because we were all repulsive in some way. We didn't really fit in anywhere else. Some of us tried, but failed. So how douchy would it have been for us to exclude W. R. for the exact same reason that we were all being excluded everywhere else?

W. R. did bring something to the group. He brought his talent and skill as an actor and as a member of the back crew. He taught us all things, and his antics made us laugh. Until he started to get annoying. B. G. very quickly lost patience with him, but Scott and I didn't actually have much self-confidence or self-respect so W. R. stayed in the group. Sadly he caused a bunch of rifts within our social dynamics that didn't become apparent until much later.

When we started high school we all saw it as a great new beginning. We were all staying together and going to one of the oldest educational institutions in the entire Salt Lake Valley: Jordan High. More on why it's so great later. Scott and I attended orientation together in a very similar way as to how B. S. and I did in middle school. The only difference was Scott's dad joined us instead of his mom.

Seriously people cut the damn apron strings! Your kids are smarter than you think, and they can handle themselves reasonably well. So what are you going to do anyway, hold their hand their entire life? Everybody grows up sometime, unless you like having a 35 year-old overweight loser in your basement; just a thought. Anyway back to orientation…

We sat in the school's auditorium with a good amount of the other incoming sophomores; in Utah sophomores are the lowest grade in a high school the freshmen are the highest grade in the middle schools. Scott and I were looking over what classes we were going to take. I was excited, I like learning. Scott however was very nervous. He said to me, "Richard, I don't know if I can do this. What if I fail?"

I attempted to calm him down and replied simply, "I won't let you." And I did make good on that promise. School started. Classes started. A new social order began to form as the students from 2 major middle schools began to merge together. The new possibilities were endless as they always are in a new environment. Groups and cliques rose and fell like small African republics. I joined and left many groups, but I always stayed true to my close friends. There was one little ritual that existed was between B. G and me. B. G. would often arrive just a few seconds after me. As I walked down the main hall of Jordan High he would yell out from behind me, "Hey Dick!" People would turn around expecting a fight. I would turn around and call out, "Sup B.!" We would meet up slap five and head to the common area where our group was sitting.

It never ceased to amaze me how truly big our group of freaks and outcastes was. It started off in middle school with about five of us. By or sophomore year, it had grown to about 20 people, and by the time we were seniors it had gone through several incarnations and consisted of no less than 40 people at any given time. The scope of our influence/control included the drama department, band, choir, debate, DECA, FBLA, track and intramural sports, cheer and all the jock groups. We were so big that if we had pushed for it we could have had a seat on the student council. But well, we were idiots. You know teenagers, and as anyone who is in high school will tell you—school sucks.

It is through this group that all the great and legendary events that happened to my friends and I happened. The guys like me, Scott, Vairin had our things like poker nights and the girls had their stuff which none of us guys understood of course.

Beginning in our sophomore year we started making movies. They were horrible. The first movie we made was for a film festival at the school. It was called *A Bad Kabuki Film Gone Bad*. It *technically* had a plot. It was however unscripted and really poorly shot. It starred me as a kabuki warrior that was in bad movie and brought to life by mixing party food and static electricity. Scott was one of the teenagers that brought me to life and my first kill. B. G. was the other teenager along with his actual little brother. I killed them too. B. G. was killed last and was sent up to Heaven where he met the Voice of God played by me. The warrior eventually died by stepping on an electric cord in the snow. While I was on camera, Scott was the Voice. The whole thing was stupid and funny. We thought we had gold on film. So the film was submitted and we went to the movie night. We waited patiently through the jocks and their horrible, violent and bloody plotless beast. Then came other atrocities and sins against the cinematic arts that I can't even remember they were so bad. So the three of us waited and waited for our film. It was not shown, and we were not notified as to why. When we asked why a violent and bloody thing and various other things that made no sense were allowed in and ours wasn't we were told a very simple fact: we had mentioned God.

Their explanation for this was mentioning God in school is against the law because then all gods would have to be allowed in from all religions and there were just too many. We knew that was a lame excuse because the administrator that had okayed all movies was Mormon just like most of the school, and we didn't say what god it was and she was inferring that it was not only the god of Christianity but of Mormonism as well. The more we pressed the issue, the angrier the administrator became until she threatened us with suspension if we did not leave her office. We folded and left. I think she just didn't like us and she just wanted to glorify the jocks, which seems to be a theme in most high schools.

As our sophomore year came to a close a new player joined our merry little band. His name was Jon, short for Jonathan of course. He was something else. Originally from Nantucket, Jon had moved to Utah a few years ago when his parents had converted the family to Mormonism and had been ostracized by their original pastor and basically kicked out of their little New England town. See it goes both ways; you didn't think of that did you? Anyway he had gone to the other middle school called Eastmont and had operated in the background up until the last month of tenth grade. Scott brought him into the group as he naturally did so often and I was thus introduced to a guy that looked a lot like a certain English wizard that wears glasses and has a scar on his forehead.

Jon became very important to me very quickly. The reason is actually very selfish and I'm not proud of it. Because of the hell that I had gone through in grade school and the joy that I had experienced in middle school, I was determined to make sure that no one could ever hurt me again. So I decided that I would be worshipped much like that movie about the high school kid that takes the day off and everybody thinks he is sick and dying. To accomplish this goal I knew I would need very good friends, because I was going to build an empire. Given my Italian heritage I decided to pattern it after Rome. I would be Caesar. B. G. would be my Pompey. Scott would be my Cato and Vairin my Cicero. So all I needed was a Cassius; I found that in Jon.

Jon was rich. Not only did he physically resemble that wizard, but his home looked like the very school in which that same wizard had his adventures. Jon seemed to want for nothing. He had everything the rest of us only dreamed about. When I first walked into his house I didn't think that I had enough money to be standing there let alone be his guest or even friend. You see society had taught me by this time that friendship was a commodity to be bought and sold like so many pieces of wood. I honestly believed that with Jon, we as a group with me at the head could become extremely powerful. I thank God to this day that I was wrong.

As I got older and wiser and the imperial dreams that I had slowly faded away, I realized that I had made a horrible mistake with my friends. It culminated in a conversation between me, Jon and Vairin during our junior year. It is also one of the few events that I can say I honestly remember. We were sitting in a hallway in the school during a break from a practice of some sort. I was exhausted and high on sugar to keep my eyes open. I said to my friends, "You guys have heard me talk about the empire right? Promise you won't tell anybody, but you are that empire. I became your friend because I wanted power, but I learned that you are that power. Any relationship built on a lie is no relationship at all. Can you forgive me?"

They did.

My junior year was one of the worst times in my life. The same went for B. G. and Scott. I was dating a girl that was poison to me. B. G.'s home almost completely fell apart. Scott was severely depressed due to strife with his parents and was taking anti-depressants as a result. Those are 3 damn good reasons for me not to remember much of that year. What I do remember about my life at this time is best told in another section because of who it revolves around. I sadly do not remember much about B. G.'s turmoil, but I had a front row seat for Scott's. While I cannot relay all that happened that year I will say this for certain: all three of us at one time attempted suicide, and at least one of us was there to pull his brother out. I say "brother" not "friend" because when someone saves your life it creates a bond that can never be broken and is stronger than blood. That is something that only men who have served in the military can possibly understand.

One thing that I do remember though is the making of our first feature length movie. It was called *A Bad Kabuki Film Gone Bad Part II* or *Kabuki II* for short. We made it as part of an assignment for theatre class. It was roughly an hour long, poorly written, decently directed, and was loaded with inside jokes, film references and pirated music and footage. Holy crap was it bad, but we were damn proud of it. I played the warrior turned demon that imprisons unsuspecting people in a dilapidated VCR and tortures them for his amusement. Scott and B. G. played those unsuspecting kids that mistakenly buy the VCR to watch movies on and get sucked in. Jon played their friend that tries to get them out but gets sucked in too and eventually becomes my slave after I kill him. While I don't want to go into the whole plot, such as it was, we basically taught ourselves how to make a film. Scott did most of the camera work and editing. I did the fight choreography. W. R. and Vairin did some of the editing and assisted Scott with the camera. Several of our friends had cameos and even Scott's girlfriend and B. G.'s girlfriend had supporting roles. As bad as it was, it was ours and the movie supplied us with enough jokes to last for several years.

After the year of hell that was my junior year was over and our lives were once again ours we as a group decided to celebrate. The celebration was called "the end of the world". I had come up with the name in the eighth grade when I had finally started listening to rock music instead of just country and heard a song that mentioned such a thing as the world ending feeling great about it. We had done it since the eighth grade. Basically on the night after the last day of school we would all get together, open some root beers, burn the remainder of our homework, reminisce and then play cards. This year was a little different. I brought my AP biology book to burn; ironic now that I think about it and what my life has become. I can remember watching each individual page of that bio book go up and saying goodbye to hell. We all raised a can to our survival and spoke blessings on what the new year was to bring.

That night an acquaintance and I took off for the desert for a yearly secret tradition of Jordan High called Senior Sunrise. This was about as close to a real kegger as you could get in Utah with a bunch of Mormon kids. And yes there was beer, but not many of us drank. The idea behind it was this was the earliest time when we were seniors. This was something all of us had been waiting for since we had known what a senior was. Given that I was a bit of a nerd as were my friends not that big of a deal. For the "cool kids" this was a make or break party. Many had their first taste of alcohol and sex that night, but us "good kids" just sat around the camp fire talking. It was here that I got to know J. D.

J. D. was a transfer student from some school further north I think Hillcrest. He was brought in by B. G. and soon started dating B. G.'s ex-girlfriend S. B. (B. G. was at the time dating her best friend A. W. she was the one in *Kabuki II*). J. D. was a poker shark, and a perv. His addiction made my addiction look tame, and actually propagated mine because it made me think that I wasn't addicted to anything. J. D. was almost the anti-W. R. When I had enough of hanging out with the super-nerd I called up J. D. and we would hang out. Our relationship continued without any major events until he graduated from high school, married S. B. and joined the army as a programmer. He is currently still married to S. B. they have one or two kids, and live in Germany.

The first part of senior year was…interesting. Scott had a really rough time. It had been a year since his parents had divorced, so B. G. and I had decided that for his birthday we would take him out to dinner at a Chinese buffet we had found in Midvale. The plan was get out of class, finish the homework quickly and then go out. We were not expecting 2 air planes to fly into the Twin Towers in Manhattan. Scott had actually stood on top of the towers the previous summer on a pilgrimage to the Ghost Fire House. He did say that he had felt sick up there and it wasn't from the gentle sway of the buildings; he just couldn't put his finger on it. At dinner that night, my two friends and I sat listening to a loop of news coverage about the attack and eating really salty food. B. G. and I did our best to cheer Scott up, but it seemed pointless.

Sometime during our senior year likely in the spring, Scott got an idea called the "other world". In my opinion this was one of his dumber ideas. One Saturday night while I was at work Scott, Vairin, B. G., S. G. (no relation), and Jon got together and had an adventure. I didn't hear about it until the following Monday at school when I walked into the school commons and saw S. G. curled up in a ball on the floor and rocking back and forth. So I asked Scott, "What's with S. G.?"

"Something happened to him."

"Scott what did you do to my student?!"

"I didn't do anything, it was the cop."

"Cop?"

"Yeah we, uh, almost got arrested Saturday night."

"What the hell did you do?!"

"Have I ever told you about the 'other world'?"

"No," I said cocking an eye brow.

“Well I had this idea that we never really are in an intersection, we only just pass through it. So I figured that if we just stood in the middle of the intersection it would be like another world.”

“Are you high?”

“You know that’s exactly what the cop said when I told him what we were doing.”

“Okay, what exactly happened?”

“Well, me, Jon, Vairin, B. G. and S. G. were hanging out while you were at work on Saturday and we got bored. So I suggested the ‘other world’, and we went out and did it where Sego Lily and Beetdigger cross.”

“The light in front of the school?”

“Yeah, it was kind of neat. It was like 2 AM. No cars were around so we decided to lie down in the middle of the intersection. S. G. and Jon didn’t like the idea, but they did it anyway. After about a minute we started to relax and everything felt fine. I said, ‘See guys nothing to worry about.’ Then the siren went ‘whoop’. We all jumped up and ran.

“The spot light hit us and the cop yelled out, ‘Stop!’ So we stopped and slowly walked back over to him.

“‘So why did you run?’ the cop asked.

“Jon said, ‘Well you did scare us.’

“He ordered us to hand over our IDs. As he was checking them he asked why we were out at 2 AM lying down in the middle an intersection. And everyone looked at me. So, I told the cop about the other world and he looked at me like you did, like I was nuts and asked if I was high. I told him I wasn’t, but he didn’t seem to believe me. Then he asked S. G. for his ID. S. G. didn't have his ID on him."

"What about his school ID?" I asked.

"He doesn't carry it with him."

"Wait doesn't S. G. have a driver's license?"

"Nope, his parents won't let him have one until his grades get better, and that's probably not going to happen."

"So what happened to S. G.?"

"He got frisked…thoroughly. The cop grabbed…him."

"I see. Do you think he'll be okay?"

Scott just shrugged.

S. G. eventually came out of his trance, but he was never quite the same after that.

The rest of senior year was largely uneventful as far as my friends were concerned. But change was coming, and it was big. It was called college and missions. As I said before I did not go on a mission like most of my friends did, instead I went to college. However you might not understand exactly what a "mission" is.

A mission is a 2 year period served by young men aged 19 to 21 years and young women aged 21 to 23 years in a "foreign" land where they work for the Church by preaching the gospel according to the prophets of Mormonism and at least attempt to make conversions. Missionaries are not compensated by the Church unless the situation is dire. Missionaries are expected to pay their own way and take care of themselves during this time. They are forbidden from entering into any relationship outside of austere friendship with the opposite sex or from holding a job. They are forbidden from engaging in any form of entertainment coming from the outside world such as television, radio, books with the exception of Church sponsored material. You for the most part cannot speak to your family or friends back home with the exception of letters/email and phone calls on religious holidays. You are given a companion who is comparatively older when you arrive in your area from a 3 week to 3 month—depending on if you are teaching in your natural tongue or not—crash course in religious studies at the Missionary Training Center or MTC. Upon completion of your first year you are now considered seasoned and given one of the newbies to teach. Most of your education is in field and you learn just about everything as you go. There is a phenomenon that occurs called the "two percent". These are missionaries that evidently turn homosexual as a result of close quarters with their companion. These individuals when caught are generally sent home in sinful shame; many commit suicide. The other 98 percent have a grand time or so I hear. They claim it is the best 2 years of their life.

All of my friends except for J. D. and W. R. and me served missions. J. D. got married and joined the army. W. R. was found "unworthy" whatever that means. And I went to college. I got into a lot of trouble for that. For each of my friends I made a celebratory "last supper"—the irony is purposeful—before they left. I made each of them something different and per their request. Scott went to the Dallas-Fort Worth area after I made him homemade pizza. Jon went to the Carolinas after I fed him a calzone. Vairin went to London,

England with my family's spaghetti sauce in his belly. B. G. went to Mexico City after a nice filling grilled steak. While most of my friends had a great time and learned a lot, B. G. almost died.

One day while he was out he ate something called street meat. I had warned him not to do this because the meat tended to be filled with parasites. His meat was; he got worms. When those things had finally left his body he got a gall bladder condition. The organ ruptured on the way to the hospital. The doctors there managed to stabilize him, but according to Church protocol he was sent home to recuperate. He came back Mexican and speaking in broken English/Spanish. I was one of the few people that could understand him. When B. G. was released from the doctor's care he was stationed in Fresno for the remainder of his mission. He came back a few weeks later with gall stones. Somehow I don't think he was supposed to be on a mission. As a result of the shame of being sent home B. G. rebelled and left the Church within no more than 2 years.

The summer before Jon left for his mission he invited me to his place for a big barbeque. Just about everybody in his family and many of his friends were there, including two girls that I knew Jon was interested in. That's right two. So in between entertaining his lady guests and his family and grilling kabobs he was feeling a little pulled. So I offered to finish cooking while he went and played. He kindly thanked me and ran off to his pool with the girls who were begging for his company. So I managed to cook the chicken kabobs on a very poor excuse for a grill and get the family fed. I left Jon's till the last; I figured I'd give him some time with the girls.

When his food was just about done I went over to the pool and said, “Hey man, food’s just about done.” He acknowledged and then went back to chasing the girls around the pool. About 5 minutes later the food was done and I was ready to eat. So I went back over to the pool to get Jon. I said, “Jon, soup’s on let’s eat.”

“Okay I’ll be right there,” and he went back to chasing the girls.

So I ate, and watched Jon have fun. As I waited for him to come get his food it was getting cold. After I finished eating, Jon was still playing so I walked back up to the pool and said, “Yo Hef, come get your food before I buy you a monogrammed silk bathrobe for your birthday.”

From that day on I called Jon “Hef” after the man himself. The thing is I call Jon that not only because the ladies love him, but because at the time he didn’t know what to do with them. For all his skill with the ladies Jon did not kiss a girl until he was 21 and back from his mission. I actually saw it happen, and I was very proud of him. Jon AKA Hef has dated a lot of girls just like his name sake; however he is a good boy. To the best of my knowledge he is single and looking for the right one, so ladies if you are interested let me know and I’ll introduce you.

While all my friends were on missions and I was in school my social life started to suffer. So I started making new friends at school. I met this one guy my freshman year that I’ll call BGR. He reminded me a lot of Scott, but there was something that I couldn’t put my figure on. So we started hanging out. We’d chat between classes and during classes that we had together, and every so often we'd go grab lunch. Then one early winter night he invited me over to his house for a game party. When I arrived there were a lot of guys and no girls, but given that he and I were both geeks I didn't think anything of it. We played a bit and I got beat pretty bad; I'm just not good at video games. So I said good night to BGR and my new friends and went home. The next week at school BGR was sitting alone in the student union and he looked sad. So I went over and asked what was wrong.

"I just got dumped," he said.

"Dumped? I didn't know you were seeing anybody. What was her name?"

"His name. I'm gay Richard."

"You're gay?! I didn't know that."

"Yeah I thought I told you."

"No you didn't."

"So does this change anything between us?" he asked.

"No it doesn't, you're still the same guy. Hey you're not interested in me are you?"

BGR looked at me like I was crazy. "No, you're not my type, and besides you are one hundred percent straight."

"Really? A lot of people think differently, how can you tell?"

"I can tell. For one thing, your sense of style is horrible. Your eyes follow boobs and girl-ass around everywhere. Then during lunch you walk in here when all the coeds are around and your tongue is on the floor. If you ain't straight you are in some serious denial. And by the way if you want to get a girl you need to fix those things."

So as a show of a good friend, BGR gave me a sense of style; namely I was not allowed to wear a baseball cap ever again, and I have not worn one since. I became much more respectful of women; the problem was I still didn't know who I was and it showed to the ladies thus ensuring my place in the legion of single losers.

The rest of my social life during college revolved around W. R. and separately with three girls and their group of friends. I actually met one of the girls at school. Hanging out with W. R. was to put it nicely…toxic. He had the strange ability to destroy self-esteem by just being there. And the older he got the fatter, uglier, and more obnoxious he became.

By the time my other friends had returned from their missions I had gone from being a good old boy with a healthy head of hair to being, well a loser with male-pattern baldness. Suffice it to say, I didn't go out much. I am convinced that had I been smart enough and had enough self-respect to not hang out with W. R. my college experience would have been a lot different. It was great. I treasure all three-and-a-half years, but they could have been better—a lot better. I don't blame W. R. Blaming him would be like getting mad at a river for running its banks, it happens. I instead blame myself, for not handling it. All the warning signs were there, I just didn't listen.

The return of my friends from their missions changed things drastically. Most of my friends with the exceptions of Vairin and B. G. of course had become very religious. I had recently found a word for what I believed, and sadly it was heretical according to the religion that I had come from. I was expecting each of my old relationships to crumble. The only one that I can say did fall apart was S. G. due to a marriage.

I remained friends with all my friends despite the changes I had made to myself, I did expect things to go back to how they were in high school. Unfortunately my rowdy friends were starting to settle down. S. G. got married. Vairin got married then divorced after the birth of his daughter. Jon and Scott moved in together and started school. I graduated college and started massage school and started to lose touch with my college friends. B. G. started to change which I didn't realize until we went to Vegas together.

My parents had bought a timeshare on the south end of the Strip. B. G. and I were both card players, and he could talk some girls into coming with us so it was on. I was expecting the girls to drive down with us, but they had work and couldn't make it as soon. So I picked B. G. up early in the morning and we set out. We got to the condo, grabbed some food and started to make ourselves at home. B. G. had recently started drinking because he was no longer Mormon. He offered me a rum and coke. I accepted. I was checking my email and didn't pay attention to what I was drinking. I took a big gulp of straight rum, but I didn't notice that it was just rum until I stood up and the room moved. I asked B. G. what he put in my drink. He said he might have forgotten to put coke in my rum and coke. Had I been able to tell which was the real B. G., I would have killed him.

The rest of the trip went just fine with the exception of the girls being too young to really go anywhere and then B. G. taking them to a musical and leaving me to go gamble by myself. B. G. and I didn't talk much after that for whatever reason. I'm sorry to say, but to date my old friend has become addicted to alcohol and poker. He is largely gone from my life.

When Scott returned from his mission I waited for a while before I started teasing him again. I have always messed with Scott; it has in a way been a defining feature of our friendship. I did it because Scott has always been kind of naive and gullible. For instance in 1999 a countdown clock was released as a festive item for the new millennium; it counted down until midnight of December 31 and then became a regular clock. Scott didn't know that. So one day when we were at my place having lunch, he looked at the clock and said, "That's weird it's counting down. Hey what happens when it reaches zero?"

I replied without even thinking, "It explodes."

The look on his face was priceless. He actually believed me. All throughout school I would tease Scott. I would untie his shoes in class, tap him on the opposite shoulder and walk away, finger on the shirt up to the nose trick, and then I would just say stuff to mess with his head. I did it so that when he got out into the real world he would be prepared for the liars and cheats that would undoubtedly cross his path. He was and still is my best friend and something of a brother to me; I had to look out for him the best way that I could.

I have actually been messing with Scott for as long as I have known him, and I decided to escalate when he got back from his mission. I would call him up randomly and ask for his phone number. I would even text him random things like, "Message M133. The subscriber you are trying to reach is unavailable. Please try your call again later." He texted me back almost immediately very confused. Lately I haven't done as much because Scott is kind of grown up now, so I figure he'll be fine.

After Jon got back from his mission he moved to his parents' new place in downtown Salt Lake City. The place was within view of the Salt Lake City Mormon Temple and the State Capitol Building. This is significant because for a time both Vairin and Scott were Jon's roommates. Hilarity often ensued. Jon and Scott fought like an old married couple. In fact for a time the joke in the group was they were actually married and Jon was the wife; Scott saddled him with that moniker. There is a story about the three of them, but because of the subject it is best suited for later.

There were some excellent parties that happened at that place. They were loaded with girls; Jon is our Hef after all. The thing is most if not all of the girls were Mormon so hooking up was out of the question. There was no alcohol and no drugs, but that does not preclude the fun we had. The parties would often go until 2 or 3 in the morning, and staying the night was always an option. W. R. did attend many of the parties, and yes he did spoil them. But the rest of the guests were awesome.

As I said before Jon resembles a certain boy wizard, and it was at this house that he got a matching scar on his forehead. Here's the story. Compared to me Jon is tall; he's a little over six feet. The houses in downtown Salt Lake City are old and built for people about my size; five-foot-six. This has nothing to do with evolution, people just eat better now and can grow quicker when they're young. Being like most young men, Jon liked to make an entrance into the basement; he however misjudged the distance one day and smacked his head on the top of the doorway. The blow knocked him out, cut him and gave him a pretty decent concussion. Of course he did finally get his scar and a good story to tell the ladies.

The first apartment that Vairin got was a horrible two-bedroom place in the "slums" of Sandy, Utah. On the north wall he put up a gigantic dry erase board, which he dubbed "the random wall". On this wall we wrote down all our inside jokes new and old and whatever else came to mind. It was awesome. One of the main features of this wall was of course Scott. He would say the most sexually explicit things and some of the dirtiest sexual innuendos with complete innocence. This earned him the nickname "innuendo man". He would say things like:

- "I'm carrying RJ's junk." RJ was a friend of ours that Scott had made on his mission. During the time of the random wall RJ and Vairin were roommates.
- "I see a cock." This is in reference to a bottle of ginger beer that Vairin had bought and left in the fridge. The bottle had a rooster on the label.
- "I tried to say 'appendage' and 'excrement' came out." Scott apparently had a mild case of turrets that day.

- "I'm taking advantage of everything, NO NOT HER."
- "I'm working on getting off." Not what you think, you pervs.
- "I'm buying you a Richard or an emu."
- "I'm thinking of things to do with my lips."
- "Are you rolling it from both ends?" I wasn't there for this one, but I do know for a fact that this was not in reference to pot.
- And last but not least "Cocking a feel." Scott actually thought that this was the term. Seriously, we had to tell him that was not the case for about 10 minutes.

The stuff he would say was almost like he was some kid from a tiny European country, who didn't know much English, and had come to the States for school and started hanging out with a bunch of crazy frat boys. He maintains that name to this day through no fault of his own.

Scott was not alone in this random wall thing. I had a few; Vairin had a few; Jon had a few and so did other people. Everything that was on the random wall was eventually erased when the wall was taken down when Vairin moved. The stuff that was written on it was preserved in a book that I believe is with either Vairin or his old roommate RJ.

Scott, Jon and Vairin are still in contact with me. We have continued to have our adventures with some very neat ones happening after I moved to Los Angeles.

MY THREE-EYED WORLD

I am a psychic. Just so there is no confusion as to what that means I will explain.

A psychic is a person that has the ability to see, understand and hear things better than other people naturally do. This includes a myriad of many abilities. Such as seeing ghosts/spirits, talking with said entities, seeing into the past, seeing into the non-local present, seeing into the future, and doing some fairly incredible stuff. There was a TV show that went off the air in 2010 because it was getting redundant and was an obvious rip off of a very popular comic. Every single person on that show that had abilities was a psychic technically speaking.

I say that because if you can understand how to do something like say fly then it's easy. That includes throwing fire and lightning (pyrokinesis and electro-kinesis), picking things up without touching them (telekinesis), knowing and understanding languages that haven't been heard or even learned by and individual, etc. All these things are possible, and according to quantum theory must happen in some fashion. I am actually writing a book on this very thing; I'm planning on it being my doctoral thesis.

I'm sure you're dying to know if I'm psychic what my abilities are. Well, I'm post-cognitive. That means I can see the past such as I can walk into a room and watch events unfold there that happened years before. I can view remotely which is the ability to see things not in the immediate vicinity. Such as I can kind of see what someone is doing on the other side of town as long as I can get a good connection. I am pre-cognitive. That means I can see into the future. However, it is technically uncertain. I can only see what could be or what will likely be. For example there is a prophecy that humanity will be gone by 2100. I checked this myself by projecting myself to 2114 and there were people there but they were hazy and without color, which I took to mean that the future is uncertain. I have seen some stuff happen before it happened and I was right within about 80 or 90 percent which is my best. I average somewhere in the eighties.

I can talk to ghosts and spirits. There is a difference. Ghosts have not crossed over. Spirits have crossed over and have come back to do something whatever it may be. There are no evil ghosts, that distinction isn't possible; they do get rather angry though. I have even crossed a few over; I got some really cool stories about that.

When I do talk to spirits I make sure that I get who I am looking for. I never ever use Ouija, those things are EVIL and nothing but bad ever comes out. I have very set protocols for contacting the other side to insure that I only speak with good spirits. Please listen to me on this: playing around with the spirit world is dangerous. There is a lot of stuff there and it is way cool at first then bad stuff starts to happen if you don't know what you're doing. And it's stuff that can drive you completely insane if you're lucky.

I can heal with a touch of my hand, and see what is wrong with a person by looking at them in various ways. This is actually my main ability and a central reason to why I have chosen medicine as my career. I can absorb energy and dispense energy. By the way, don't do that it's surprisingly dangerous. I can understand all the elements. How that came to be is an excellent story, but first how I came to know what I am.

When I was a kid of about 4 years I had a dream. Actually it was more like a nightmare from the imagery, but I was not scared at all; I was focused. It started out with me sitting on the front step of my house and seeing M. J. from across the street walk into the house next to him along with his older brother and a couple of other kids from down the street. The house looked different than before, it seemed alive and angry. They knocked on the door, it opened and they were sucked in. I bolted across the street to the house and forced the door open. The entry way was different than it should have been. It was instead what I would now call Pre-Victorian. The room was circular in shape. The walls and floor were covered in a red carpet with a gold leaf design. On my left rose a dark mahogany curving staircase that went up to an open balcony. At the top of the staircase stood a man. He was dressed completely in black and very stylish. He had no hair on his head not even eyebrows, and he had the most terrifying red eyes that I have ever seen. He smiled down at me; it made my skin crawl. As he started down the staircase he said to me, "Welcome, I've been expecting you."

I said to him, "Who are you, and where are my friends?"

"Don't worry they're fine. You'll be joining them soon."

Suddenly long, black, gooey tentacles with claw-like graspers shot out from the walls at me. They grabbed me and pulled me to the far wall away from the door. I was pinned with my back to the wall and the tentacles wrapping around me. I said to the man, "You won't get away with this."

He came closer to me and I saw my friends now changed into hideous creatures standing behind him. He said to me, "Of course I will. I wanted you most of all."

I screamed out, "NO!" And I ripped through my bonds. The man was stunned to see this happen. I reached behind me into my back pocket and pulled out a cannon made out of gold and turned it on one of my friends. When the round hit him he turned back into himself. I said to him, "Get help," and I continued to shoot the creatures that were now coming into the room. Each of the creatures that I shot turned back into a normal person. Angels arrived and started helping out. The man had retreated, but we found him and destroyed him. We laid waste to the house and razed it the ground. After saying goodbye to my friends, I woke up sweating.

The following morning I told my mom about the dream. She seemed very concerned and started to ask me very direct questions, which I answered very truthfully being that I was four. Then she asked me if I was okay. I felt fine just a little shaken. She was very proud of me and told me that I was very special, and that the dream had actually happened and that I had saved some people that night. Later that day I overheard my mom talking on the phone with someone while I was playing. I of course don't remember all of what she said, but I do remember her saying, "Do you think he is one? I agree, then I will begin." My life changed that day.

For the next 4 years or so my mom took me to church almost every single week. We studied scripture together in a way that I could understand, and I really enjoyed it. I was hanging out with my mommy. Who wouldn't love that? She made sure I understood everything about the Bible, but for some reason the Book of Mormon was a bit neglected. This is odd because we were Mormon. I guess my mom sensed something about me, but allowed it to play out as needed.

During this time I was spending a lot of time with my grandpa. We were close to say the least. He took me to the zoo. He and my dad built me a train set. He was awesome. Then when I was about 6 or 7, something happened. I'm naturally very quiet, and I have been known to sneak up on my cat. I did something stupid and snuck up on my grandpa; he was an ex-soldier and kind of jumpy. I wrapped my arms around his legs and pressed my face into his back. The next thing I knew I was on the other side of the room with a burning sensation on my head. My grandpa had backhanded me and sent me across the room because I had spooked him. From then on things between the two of us were different. I was very cautious around my grandpa now, I made sure to only approach him from the front and at that make sure he saw me first. He also started becoming very forceful and impatient with me. He never hit me again, but I guess I could tell he was restraining himself.

Why does some odd abuse from my grandfather have anything to do with my being a psychic? My grandpa is also psychic. However he never really learned how to use what he has. In a way, I wear my mask but his mask wears him. About the time he backhanded me was about the time my abilities started to develop, and I started to see things that weren't just part of my imagination. He did not know about this; my mom hadn't told him anything. So it seems that subconsciously my grandpa viewed me as a threat.

A short time later, my grandpa became very paranoid. He started believing that the government was after him and that he was some sort of re-incarnation of a great Nephite general or something and that Bigfoot was real, etc. My dad kicked him out of the house rather violently one night, and forbade him from having any contact with me or my mom ever again. We, my grandpa and I, have not been on good terms since that night.

During this time as well I had a fear of the dark, but it was only in a certain section of my house—the hallway from the bathroom to my bedroom, and in the basement directly underneath. This was the reason: our house was haunted. Starting when I was about five, every night when I went down to my room to get ready for bed I would see the white silhouette form of a person with big black glowing eyes. All I could feel from this thing was hate. So I learned to turn on the hall light and sprint down the hall to my bedroom. This drove my sister nuts. She thought that I was just some dumb kid that was starved for attention and that I should stop turning the light on because it was making it hard for her to go to bed.

So my dad sat me down and had a talk with me. He asked me if I was actually seeing what I said I was seeing or if I was just playing games. I told him that I was actually seeing it and I begged him to believe me. He evidently did, because a priest was called to bless the house and attempt to get rid of the ghost. It worked for a few days, and then the ghost attacked me. One night when I went to go to bed I decided to keep the light off. Right as I got passed the bathroom the ghost appeared in front of me. It was a woman; she was livid. I couldn't exactly hear her voice, but her face and the words that she was forming with her mouth terrified me. I called for my mom and dad and they came running. They found me in the hall transfixed and liquid paper white. They grabbed me and asked what happened. All I could say was, "It's a lady, and she is very mad at me."

The priest obviously didn't work. So my mom called our bishop to do something similar as to what the priest did. He sat down with us and we told him what was going on. He seemed skeptical, until he talked to me. My bishop saw the fear in my eyes and decided that it was real. He started the prayer to bless the house, and the house started to shake a little. I opened my eyes and saw the lights starting to flicker. As the prayer continued the lights and the shaking of the house became more pronounced. My mom grabbed me and held me tightly. Right at the end of the prayer I heard the muffled scream of a woman come from down the hall, and then silence.

I don't remember who spoke first, but there was a kind of peace in the house that I had never felt before. We said our goodbyes and thanks to my bishop. My mom, dad and I sat down to talk; my sister was out on a date. My mom asked my dad, "So how did she die? Tell your son."

My dad then proceeded to tell me about his first wife named Lisa. They had actually bought the house together, and she was very adamant about getting this particular house. Not long after they had moved in she got pregnant, and things seemed to be going perfectly. Then Lisa got sick with a respiratory condition that ended her life in the hallway of the house between my bedroom and the bathroom. The cause of death was fluid in the lungs. About 2 years later my parents got married and I was born.

The thing about Lisa is this. She was a ghost that did not know she was dead. She thought that her and my dad were still married and that my dad was cheating on her with my mom and had a bastard child with her, which is why she was always so mean to me. We had to convince her she was dead to get her to cross over and end not only her torment but mine as well.

About a year later my mom told me about a dream she had the night before. She was back in high school in the 1970's and dressed in the kind of hippie way that she did. She walked into the cafeteria which was empty except for the usual chairs and tables and Lisa. Lisa was sitting at one of the tables dressed in a similar style to my mom. You see, my mom and Lisa had actually gone to school together. As my mom entered the room Lisa stood up and motioned for my mom to come closer. When my mom got closer she said, "Lisa what are you doing here?"

"There is something that I need to talk to you about. Would you have a seat?"

My mom and Lisa sat down. Lisa seemed very remorseful.

My mom asked, "Is everything okay?"

"No. I did something really bad to you and your son. I was very sick, and that is no excuse for how I acted. Can you please forgive me?"

My mom realized what was happening. "Yes I can. I forgive you."

They stood together and hugged, and then my mom woke up.

As I continued to grow, my religious studies began to expand. By the time I was 10 I knew the Bible forwards and backwards, which is better than now by the way. I knew what tribes had been taken by the Assyrians and what had been conquered by the Babylonians. I could tell you who a given prophet was just by his description. As I said before I knew things when I got baptized at 13 that the missionaries didn't know and at a level that was in effect scholarly. I was still a little hit or miss on the Book of Mormon, so I started going to church and I made friends with the returned missionaries that hadn't gotten married yet.

One day in Sacrament Meeting, I was watching one of the chief church leaders give a talk about the importance of something for something, that's irrelevant anyway. The missionary that I was sitting next to heard me snicker. He assumed that I was making fun of the big wig at the podium and prepared to scold me. He asked me why I was laughing. I said that there is a guy with a long white beard standing next to the speaker and whispering in his ear. I thought this was hilarious. The missionary looked at me like he had seen something that shouldn't exist. I told my mom about what had happened that day at church and she told me to never again say anything like that again to anybody else. I could get into a lot of trouble. When I asked why, my mom told me that according to the Church's laws that they believed people like me were evil and they might take me away. Her telling me this made me very guarded and mistrustful of people around me, and would characterize my social life for years to come.

I continued to age and grow and mature, and so did my abilities. As I got better at what I did I also became more mistrustful of people around me. The resulting depression was stifling. All psychic abilities hinge on the emotional state of the psychic, and mine was less than stellar. I didn't lose my abilities, but they did start to change. They became very coarse, and I wanted to weaponize them. I just couldn't figure out how until I came across sorcery. I started to study the ancient art and to design spells. Then something happened to me that in retrospect was a good thing. I got yelled at and grounded by my mother. She told me that this was not the way of our kind, and that if I ever started doing anything like this ever again she would put me in a hole so deep that I would never claw my way out. I abandoned magic after about 2 months' time. I was 11 years old.

The following year in sixth grade sometime in the spring I was playing basketball with some classmates at recess. One of the guys, A. S., wasn't playing his best which was odd because he was the star athlete of the school. I asked him what was wrong. He said he had a stomachache. So I put my hand on his belly and said "heal" under my breath. My hand got really hot and tingly. A. S. suddenly stood up straight and said, "Wow that actually feels better, thanks."

I had never done that before, but somehow I knew what to do. I told my mom what I had done. She said, "Good, now I can start teaching you." My mom didn't know much about projection, but she did know about ghosts and prayer and divination. She started to teach me all of these things with the first being astrology. She taught me what each of the signs and planets were, but I didn't really know how to use it until I was in college some time later. She started to teach me numerology; again I came into it in college. So why did it take me at least seven years to learn how to use the stuff that my mother was teaching me? I just had other things on my mind like school, girls, work and Aikido.

At the start of my seventh grade year I started getting into fights with this kid that just loved to push my buttons. So my mom called an old friend of hers who was a sensei of Aikido and enrolled me in classes. I will go into more detail later, but the training provided gave me a calm that I had never known. He also noticed that I was different from the other students.

I picked things up without practicing. I could perform a technique after having only been shown it a few times. I seemed to be able to know my opponent's move before he did. So my sensei took me aside and did some testing on me. He took out a small whistle and blew it. I covered my ears and begged him to stop. Then he told me to close my eyes and sniff the air. I did as I was told and was able to correctly identify the scent from across the room. Then he asked me if I turned on the lights when I was at home. I told him only if it's really dark which doesn't usually happen. Then he asked if I had a burning sensation in my forehead ever. All the time. He smiled and said that he was going to teach me something special.

He set me with the senior class and ordered them to attack me. I figured it was going to be just a bit of group sparring. I was wrong. He first bound my eyes and my ears. I had to defend myself on smell alone. It took a little while but I managed to figure it out. Then he plugged my nose and opened my ears. The students were ordered to move very quietly; they may as well have been a marching band. Night time rolled around and I was given my eyes, but nothing else and with the same results. We only did one more session, but the results were amazing. To this day I can tell the difference between many different smells from several feet away, hear my cat walk across the floor and see in the dark.

In addition to this I was taught how to work with energy. My sensei taught me how to scan a room and identify varied pockets of energy. He taught me how to form and manipulate energy such as forming a sphere between my hands and setting a pool of energy in one hand and changing its shape. He taught me better how to use my healing ability, and how to weaponize it if necessary. He taught me that magic was just the art of knowing how to manipulate energy and matter, and thus all things were possible. The next day at school I decided to try out the idea. I was standing in the lunch line waiting for my chance to get crappy food. I closed my eyes and thought of being lighter than air. It took me about 2 minutes, but my heels actually lifted off the floor. I realized what I had done and decided that I was different enough and to not do that again. I have not been able to do it since.

As part of my training my sensei advised me to create a psychic means to defend myself. I took this to mean I needed weapons and armor. So I meditated and fashioned my own armaments out of my own energy. I had a smooth Spartan style helmet with matching breastplate, Roman Legion style skirt and pants, French renaissance era grieves, English archer gauntlets, Spanish sailing boots, and a long blue cape tied in front with a gold chain. My weapons included a Japanese katana, a German officer's pistol, an English longbow, an Italian stiletto, and an Irish round shield. I was decked out. Had all this gear actually existed it would have weighed at least 100 pounds. I was completely insane. What is worse I actually thought it was a good idea and I started to use these weapons.

As I said before, it was about this time that Scott and I began to become really good friends. The June before I left for Nashville we were talking about ghosts and about his hobby involving the show about capturing ghosts. He told me that he didn't like to go into the clubhouse that his dad had built for him and that it always gave him the creeps. I decided we should go check it out. Scott grabbed his camera and we headed outside to the clubhouse. He opened the door and turned on his camera so that he could see what I could see at a later time. I scanned the room and found a pocket of energy by the door, and it was moving. I made the assumption that this was a demon; after all I had been taught by the Church that these things existed and were working tirelessly to either turn us good church folk evil or kill us. So I examined the energy pocket and decided that it was a serpent of some kind. I looked closer and it started to take shape. The form that it took was that of a viper with big jaw on the bottom and long fangs jutting up. Its eyes were in the usual spot but blood red. Instead of having scaly skin it had an exoskeleton. I told Scott we had to leave, and as I was closing the door and repeating a barrier spell that I had learned I felt a stinger enter my shoulder.

We rushed inside and examined the tape and I showed Scott what we were facing. All the while a felt a sharp pain growing in my neck and shoulder. I started to get light headed, so Scott and I decided that we had to take care of the problem before it got out of hand. The meditation that we did was intense. Scott managed to pull out the “stinger” that was in my shoulder, and I managed to take care of the splash back on Scott’s mind. Afterword we went back outside and attacked the “demon”; I killed it.

Over the next 2 to 3 years there were 2 other battles with demons at Scott’s house. However, I now know that there were no actual entities there. They were manifestations of the discord and severe Feng Shui issues inherent in Scott’s life and my own as well.

You see, there is an odd phenomenon called “tulpa” that arises when a person or group of people believe so strongly in something that it actually happens. Demons are one of those things, as are just about every “monster” that people whole heartedly believe exist. These include vampires, werewolves, demons, Bigfoot, the Loch Ness monster, gnomes, Santa Clause, the list continues. People, these do not exist, as in they were not created by God or anything else other than a bunch of people being stupid. And by the way that includes the Devil—not real. Call me a devil for saying that, I don't care. The Devil is not real, I promise.

I have not told you the whole story about my time in Tennessee. At the Hermitage, I met someone there that didn't have a body. He seemed to be a priest. I am not sure if he was ghost or a spirit, but we talked at length for about 30 minutes. I told him the history of the United States from about 1830 to the present day. In return he gave me a warning; I was to be careful on my return home, I was weak and danger was everywhere around me. I thanked him and left. As I said before, funnel clouds followed us home the whole way. I thought I was safe when I was back in Utah, but I was wrong.

I got hit by the car a few days later, and while I was in the ambulance I saw angels. There were 6 of them I think, with wings of various colors. Some were 2 different shades of blue. One had red wings, and other white. They were the most beautiful people I had ever seen. I was told to rest and that I would be just fine; I was safe now. I remember when I told my bishop about this he got angry with me and said that angels don't have wings, and that they would never help me because I was unworthy of such assistance.

It was during this time that I started meditating. I met someone during my meditation. It was my guide or as my Christian/Mormon friends would say, the Holy Ghost. Everyone has their own; mine amazingly enough has a Hebrew name that I can't pronounce for the life of me. All I know is it starts with an H and you cough halfway through. When I first conversed with him I spent 10 minutes trying to say his name until he told me to just call him "James" before I hurt myself. I've been able to hear him ever since. Whether or not I listened to him is a different story. Case in point, bike meets car. Really should have listened that day. Now whenever I hear his voice in my right ear I listen. He is there to help me after all.

I wrote earlier about a kid named S. G. and I referred to him as my student. S. G. was like me. He was psychic, and a bit of an outcaste. So beginning in the summer before our junior year of high school I started teaching him who and what he was and how to use his abilities. The problem was we were both part of a religion that called itself "God's Army", and publicly believed everything that we were was evil.

But we persevered. I taught S. G. how to use his pre-cognitive abilities, I taught him how to focus his mind and form balls of energy in his hands and change the nature of that energy just as I had been. I even taught him how to get his own weapons and how to use them. And then I taught him about the 13 elements.

The 13 elements are something that I figured out when I was about fourteen. It was a rainy Saturday afternoon. I had no homework and nothing to do. All my friends were busy, and there was nothing on TV. I had recently come in from doing a special meditation in the thunderstorm called Ten Shin Go So (Art of Heaven and Earth). This meditation was one of the many things that my sensei had taught me. It is used to gain energy from the natural world, and to commune with the natural world. It is very loud and involves special movements and sounds. So after the meditation I was lying on the couch drying off from the rain, and feeling great. My thoughts turned to the elements: Earth, Fire, Wind and Water. I was classifying things to them, and then I realized they actually account for very little. So I went into the Chinese system of Fire, Earth, Metal, Water and Wood. Same attempt to classify and the same result of not everything fits. If a system is going to be useful then it has to be absolute or as close to absolute as possible. The Western and Eastern metaphysical element systems fail this very clearly.

So I thought, "What does an element need to be considered an element?" It has to be simple. It has to be found everywhere, and in common form at least. It also has to be recognizable in its function in the universe. Fire, Earth, Metal, Wind, Water and Wood fulfilled these requirements, but just these 6 made the universe too simple and too chaotic. Other things are needed to bring order. So I looked outside to my favorite thing in the atmosphere—the thunderstorm that was now raging. As I thought a lightning bolt streaked across the sky and a clap of thunder followed immediately behind. Of course electricity! But in other societies that identified this as a force in nature, they called it "Thunder" which actually referred to the thunderbolt (lightning). Then I thought, what about comets? They're made of ice, not just water but other stuff as well. Ice had to be an element. Over the next couple of hours I reasoned out a total of 12 of the 13 elements including Sun, Moon, Cloud and Shadow. Number 13 eluded me for quite some time. It wasn't that I wanted there to be 13 elements, I just figured that there should be 13 elements due to the pervasiveness of the number in the world. I will let you figure that out, or you can just read my book.

Originally I thought Time was an element, until I realized that according to Relativity, time is mutable and therefore fails a big test for an element. Not to mention Time is completely subjective and can only be observed if a change can be noticed. A little over a year passed and I figured that I was wrong on my logic that there were only 12 elements; still I figured out more than ever before. Then I took biology for the first time in the tenth grade. Utah schools aren't that big on science for some reason. I realized that if Wood was an element then Flesh had to be as well. I now had all thirteen!

All this time I was trying to figure out how to learn and understand the elements. At first I just meditated and I learned about one per year. But I had a student to teach and I only saw the weapon applications of the elements. I needed things to go faster. So I figured to use Ten Shin Go So. The whole point of the meditation was to exchange energy with the universe and the elements are nothing but energy. So I used it on the more pervasive elements like Water, Cloud and the like. Then I noticed a problem with elements like Fire and Earth. For them to be around me enough to learn them with Ten Shin Go So would cause me to die. So S. G. and I resorted to passive absorption by holding the element in our hands and pulling on it with our minds. Fire was the most difficult to say the least. We did manage to learn all 13 elements at least that was our belief at the time, and we decided to add them to our weapons during our practice sessions.

It has been a very long time since I was this person; he is long dead now. Leave what I studied about magic at that.

It was during my high school years that something horrible happened to a very dear friend of mine, I will call her My Stylist. I have known this woman for my entire life. Her and my parents are the best of friends. She even gave me my first hair cut. When I was a teenager she was dating a guy that got into some trouble with the local PD. He was held up in the basement of her house. The police came in and her boyfriend died from being shot. The event caused My Stylist to seek our help. My dad was once a cop and evaluated the scene, while my mom and I used our abilities to counsel and consol My Stylist. My mom got him to cross over and we purified the house. Until I came out as a psychic in my early twenties My Stylist was one of 7 people that knew what I was. As gratitude for all our help my mom, dad and I were given free haircuts for life from her. I went to My Stylist up until the day she shaved my head as per my request.

After high school all my friends including S. G. went on missions. As I said before I made new friends including Sara. It was through her that I learned a lot about myself. Sara was a psychology major, and it was about this time that I was beginning to study many different religions and to break away from the Church. When I started college I picked up everything on spirituality and metaphysics I could find. I read the Bhagavad-Gita, the Koran, a different Bible from the King James II version that I had been taught all my life the only version that should ever be read. I started to study Feng Shui, Eastern and Western Astrology, Numerology and finally the Tarot. I also started to pick up books on past-life regression. I did this because starting when I was 15 I started having dreams, nightmares mostly, about places I had never been with people I didn't know. I did things in those dreams that I had never done before. I spoke languages that I had never even heard before much less been trained in.

One of the biggest dreams involved me in a jungle. I was bigger than I am even now, and I was loaded with muscle. It was hot and humid the way it is just after a fresh rain. I was wearing a vest with a bunch of pockets on it and a very tight, heavy backpack. I had a very large rifle in my hand and I was wearing something on my head. I was walking through a clearing with a bunch of guys that were dressed a lot like me. We were looking for something. Suddenly coming from the forest I heard *Jingle Bells* playing. We all stopped. Then just as quickly as the music began, it turned to the sound of a woman screaming. I heard somebody yell out, "They're here! Fan out!" I rushed forward, rifle at the ready. I scanned the tree line for movement; I saw a fern move. I ran towards it. Then somebody wearing a big sloping hat and holding a rifle sprang up and shot me in the face. Just as the bullet hit me I woke up in a cold sweat.

I told my parents about the dream the next day. My dad joked saying that I had been hunting VC all night and one of them got me. According to my dad, I had a dream about the Vietnam War, and I died. We dismissed it as me just remembering that movie about the idiot guy that practically makes history accidentally. That interpretation changed later.

Another dream happened later that year. I was in a forest of pine trees and birches. It was cold and foggy. I was wearing a long cape and boots. I was standing beside a horse and tying something to it. I then turned around, and there was a woman standing there dressed in a cape similar to mine with the hood pulled up. She had big blue eyes that were filled with sadness, and she really didn't want me to leave her. I took her chin in my hands and kissed her. Then I said, "*Revolvare*" which means "I will return". I got on my horse and rode away. I woke up crying. I had recently learned how to draw people, so I jumped out of bed and flicked on my light. I drew the woman in the dream, and I still have that picture; only a few people have ever seen it.

It got really weird when these dreams merged into the waking world. One morning during my freshman year of college I came down to breakfast and said what I thought was in English, "Morning mom, what's for breakfast?" My mom was standing at the stove cooking and my dad was eating his oatmeal at the table. They both stopped and stared at me. My mom was holding a spatula in one hand and looking at me with her jaw on the floor. My dad stopped mid-bite and when the spoon finally fell from his hand into the bowl, I looked around the room and said, "Ka?" which means, "What?"

I didn't know what had happened. I knew what I had said; it just wasn't in English apparently. After I got to school, I spoke with one of my professors who was also a linguist. I repeated to him exactly what I had said. He looked at me and asked if I had ever spent time in Israel or Syria. I had never left the lower 48 states. Then he asked what my nationality was. Italian with some

Romanian, German and Irish. He told me that what I had said to my mom was "Good morning, what is for first meal?" in Aramaic. The Jesus movie where they used all the languages wouldn't be released for a few years yet. I had never heard this language. I knew of its existence but I didn't know anything more than that.

So you freaked out yet?

God knows I was. I told my bishop about what had happened. He told me that I was either insane or possessed and needed an exorcism immediately. He advised me to go see a psychiatrist and get diagnosed so I could start taking medication. I did not do this, because I knew I was psychic, but I didn't know what I was seeing. I got the answer 2 years later.

I had come across a book by one of my fellow psychics, she's a bit of a rock star in the metaphysical world and has been on numerous talk shows and written many books and done some very high profile things. In one of her books she details how to be hypnotized in order to reach past lives. I didn't entirely believe it, but a few things had happened recently that I will go into further in this chapter that gave me enough to go out on faith. So I grabbed my good and trustworthy friend Sara the psych major. We went to a friend's house that she was sitting for, and she hypnotized me according to my instructions. We turned the tape player on and began to record. I was taken back through a total of 9 lifetimes. I have more but these were significant enough to record.

The first one back was in the 1960's. I was a farm boy from Illinois named "Michael". I wanted to go to college with my girlfriend Kara and become a doctor, but my dad demanded that I join the army and go to Vietnam to fight the Communists. I died there from being shot in the face. That was the dream in the jungle that I had. I am convinced now that the life I'm living now is a replay of the failure of my last life with the God-given chance to fix my past mistakes. I also suspect that this is true for most of my generation; this is our second chance.

The next one back involved the Boxer Rebellion, which is something that I have always had an odd interest in. I was Korean, and had moved to China to seek better fortune. I got pulled into the war because I was protecting some young children from the evil people around; I died from being shot by a British officer in the back.

The next few are a bit foggy. I have misplaced the tape recently, so I will describe them to the best of my recollection. I was a Spanish "merchant sailor" as I said on the tape. This is code for pirate. I'm pretty sure this was in about 1540ish. Our port-of-call was Taraco, but we sailed all over the Mediterranean; we went as far east as Turkey. I had many names and this seemed to upset Sara as she interviewed me. As I listened to the tape afterward, I realized where my cockiness comes from. She finally got me to give my real name of "Diego". I died on the ship, but not in the way you might think. We were in port at home and my shipmates wanted to grab a drink at the tavern. I still had some sails to tie off on the top mast, so I told them to go on without me and I would catch up. I had bought some sheepskin gloves to protect my hands; this was a big mistake, because as I was tying off I slipped and fell all the way down the deck and landed on my neck. I became a ghost as a result. It wasn't because I had died before my time;

it was because I was ashamed that I had died the way I did. I walked around for 20 years with a bent neck following my friend Enzo until he died and I was able to crossover with him. In this current life I have suffered from an inexplicable fear of heights and neck problems.

I was an Italian nobleman in the Renaissance. I had to flee to escape intrigue and to protect my wife. It happened late at night and in the woods outside my city. This is the dream about the young woman. Whoever she was I have no clue and I don't know if I ever saw her again, but I am sorry I had to do that, and I'm sure that I could have done better.

I was a Toltec priestess, that's right I was once a woman. I had many duties including anointing the young and ritualized sex with the high priest. I couldn't stand him. To this day I do view sex as being very sacred and the woman should be happy. The town that I was part of got invaded by men wearing animal skins and moving like the animals they were wearing. I later figured out that these were Aztec jaguar warriors, and that the village had been conquered. I managed to save a few people and get them to safety, but I met my end at the stinger of a scorpion in my right ankle.

I was a Saracen merchant during the time of Saladin and Richard the Lionhearted. I actually saved a templar knight from death. His troop had been killed, he had survived. My sons and I had found him in the desert nearly dead and all alone on the way to Jerusalem. We picked him up, got him some water and some food, and saved his life. After he realized where he was and who we were he cursed me and rushed out and into the city. A couple of days later he found me being attacked by a mob for some reason, and he saved my life thus repaying his debt to me. I would meet him again a few centuries later.

I was an English farm wife during the ninth century. I was married to a man named "Tom" whom I repeatedly said was a "nice man". I guess the life was rather uneventful.

I was a tribal Dacian during the era when Greek Christians were beginning mission work in Eastern Europe. I actually asked Sara, "Who is Christ?" She stopped in surprise and said that she would ask the questions.

And finally, I was once Egyptian. I worked as a sculptor during what I'm guessing is the Middle Kingdom era. My king was good; he was kind and generous to his people. We were happy, and I was very proud of my work. I sculpted the gods. My favorite to make seemed to be Ra because I claimed that no one could do a better job. When Sara questioned me about this a got kind of defensive and said that, "My king is my god and my god is my king." I seem to have been rather militant then.

When Sara brought me out of the hypnosis, I was severely dehydrated. I had been under for a full hour and a half, and talking the whole time. I had a horrible headache, and I felt exhausted. She asked me if I believed in past lives. I said I guess so.

I do want to put a warning here. Past life regression is a good idea, if you are willing to face the hardships that you have already gone through. It does need to be with someone you trust and knows how to hypnotize you effectively. If you do this incorrectly, you can severely damage your psyche and probably drive yourself completely insane. I'm not saying don't do it, just with all things involving the mind and the other side please be careful.

As I said before, I had recently read some books that had given me a new kind of faith and allowed me to do what I did. It all started in college with a religion studies class. This was basically a survey of several different religions. In high school when I studied religions it was only the western sects of Christianity, no other forms of worship or belief were recognized at all. They were all lumped into a big bag called Paganism. When I got to college however I was briefed on the ideas behind Judaism, Islam, Christianity both Eastern and Western, Paganism/Wicca, Buddhism, Taoism, Confucianism, etc. My professor was a Baptist minister and had studied all religions in depth so as to understand them. This class was fascinating. It quickly became my favorite of the semester, and I learned something.

I learned that there was more to God than I had been told. I wanted more. It was because of this class that I started reading all the sacred works that I could get my hands on. But it wasn't enough. It was also about this time that I watched a movie that had actually been banned in Utah for its subject matter. It involves a woman who is the descendent of Jesus and her mission to prevent a couple of renegade angels from re-entering heaven. This movie made me question everything that I had been taught by the Church. This movie and my religions class made my bishop very unhappy with me, and it in a way lead to the threat he made to me that I needed to mind the consequences of my actions.

I kept reading. I found the psychic's books that I told you about earlier and devoured them. I read about the nature of good and evil, what Heaven is like, and all the mechanisms that go into existence. She did warn me to not believe anything she wrote, and to instead do the research for myself and to only take what works for me. She called this system of philosophy "Gnosticism" and the people who practice it are called, "Gnostics". It means to seek truth. The entire system is built on logic not blind faith. You make our own discoveries about God and the universe, and you bow to no one but the Creator. I thought this was awesome, so I tested it out.

She wrote about a way to talk to God in order to get proof of existence, and here's a little wrinkle: talk to God as though God were female and call Her Azna. So I did this, I called Azna out. I made sure that I was completely alone. I said my prayer and asked Her for a rose in any form that is the most convenient for delivery and I wanted it in one week's time. For the sake of continuity, let me tell you the time frame of this; it was right when that guy wrote those 2 books that take place in Italy and France about messages buried in puzzles. I had a pretty decent grasp of the sacred idea of the female goddess and Her relation to the number 5. So a week later to the day it was raining heavily as it often does in the spring time in Salt Lake City. My college had just had a festival involving fake flowers. I had a really bad day at work, and school wasn't any better; I was very depressed. Not to mention my rose had failed to materialize. So I got in my car to go home with the new and re-enforced belief that there was no Goddess and perhaps no God. Then my foot slipped as I got in my car.

I checked the bottom of my shoe, and discovered a piece of red synthetic fabric cut in the shape of a five-pointed rose. My mouth fell open in shock and awe. I stared at this simple piece of fabric for a long time, and then I smiled and said, "Wow, you're good." I looked at my watch and it was about the time that I had said the prayer the week before. Ask and ye shall receive, eh?

From that day forward I was devoted to Her. Now before the heresy alarms start going off, let me say this: I am a Christian in the sense that I follow the teachings of Jesus of Nazareth who is called Christus. Now because of my new allegiance to the Divine Mother, I decided to convert to Gnosticism. The thing is, Gnostics are quiet. In antiquity they were hunted nearly to extinction for the simple fact that they don't pay tithing to anyone. The Pope didn't like that then and still doesn't like it now, nor does the Mormon Prophet. So I laid low at first. I continued to go to church here and there while I continued to study. Eventually I couldn't take it anymore, and I just quit going.

This of course caused the Church to go into rescue mode, which is they send home teachers over to your house to in effect con you back into coming to church. I actually saw this in a movie that was released right before I quit going to church. The star of the show gets home from his mission gets married and then comes home one day to find is wife smoking a cigarette and drinking a beer. She denounces the Church and divorces him. He is sent into depression and begins to "sin" by drinking tea. Mormons aren't supposed to drink tea for some strange reason. He does some other lame things in a half-hearted form of rebellion. He starts going to a singles' ward and meets a girl there, they eventually get married. She does get after him for his job as a stand-up comic and his poking fun at the Church. The entire film was shot in Utah, and is loaded with strange jokes that are only funny if you are mainstream Mormon and understand various film references. I could not tell the difference between a joke and serious dialog in the film. My friends all thought it was great but it made no sense to me. In short the movie sucked.

I refused to hear the home teachers, and I actually found the things that they read to me and said to me to be very insulting. They did eventually get the idea that I wasn't interested anymore and only stopped by to see my mom.

I think it's time for a ghost story.

I think it was my sophomore year of college in the middle of the summer; I got off late from a bussing shift during the 24th of July Founders' Festival at a local restaurant. I got home at about 1 AM, and I was exhausted. I warmed up the leftovers from dinner that my parents had left me and fueled up. Even though I was exhausted I was still a little wired so I turned on the TV to watch some late night cable cartoons. I fell asleep on the couch for about 30 minutes. Then I heard a voice in my ear say, "Richard, you need to get up there is someone here to see you."

I opened my eyes and looked into the northwest corner of my living room from where I had been sleeping. I was amazed at what I saw. I saw the figure of a woman floating about 2 or 3 feet off the floor looking down at me. She was wearing a long white night gown that looked beautiful on her. Then I looked at her face; it was a bloody skull. Her curly brown hair was caked with blood and her night gown was stained with it down to her ribcage. As she looked at me her bony jaw moved and she said, "Can you help me?"

I looked at her completely unafraid and replied, "Yes I can. You're dead, you need to cross over. My friend James will help as will some angels."

She then disappeared along with James. I woke up the next morning and found my dad watching a special report on the news about a young woman who had gone missing. At first I thought nothing of it until her picture came across the screen. It was the woman that I had seen the night before, only with her face intact. She was beautiful. Her husband had filed a missing person's report when she had not returned from her jogging trip the previous night.

I said to my dad, "She's dead."

"How do you know that?"

"She was here last night. Her face was gone, and she was wearing a white night gown."

The case developed, and a few weeks later her body was found at the county dump rolled in a rug that she and her husband had bought together before she had disappeared. He was tried and convicted of murder. He had shot his wife in the face with a shotgun while she slept.

The following Thanksgiving weekend, I was working and I got home late again. I warmed up the leftovers my mom had left for me and I fell asleep again on the couch watching cartoons. Again I heard a voice in my ear that said, "Richard, you need to wake up there is someone here to see you."

I opened my eyes and again I looked into the northwest corner of my living room to see the same woman floating there again. There was one key difference—she was whole. She looked down at me, smiled and said, "Thank you." She disappeared in a flash of light. To date she is the only ghost that I have ever crossed over that has returned to thank me. Not that I want to be thanked at all, I'm just doing my job. The gesture is nice though.

On ghosts: please don't fear them. Some you might want to be cautious around, but please remember these are your brothers, sisters, fathers, mothers, cousins, aunts and uncles. They deserve peace, just as all of us do. If you come across a ghost please do them a favor and do all that you can to get them to cross over. Don't study them and poke at them like some science experiment, they're people dammit and they need help. Be that help.

Another instance involved me hanging out with Jon. It was late at night, and we were talking about ghosts; a subject that has always fascinated him. I asked if he would like to see a real one. He said sure. So we jumped in my car and I listened. I got a bead on a ghost about 2 miles away and we drove off. The signal as it were, led us into a cul-de-sac. Standing in the middle of the road was a young woman dressed in a pioneer era dress. My headlights shown on her and half of her body disappeared. She then walked towards us and passed through the front end of my car and came to rest in the back seat. Jon watched in awe as all this happened.

I heard her say, "Please go quickly, he's coming."

I drove off and asked her, "Can you make it on holy ground?"

"YES JUST HURRY!"

I found a church just a few blocks down the road. She was shrieking in the back seat, and making it very difficult to concentrate. Even Jon could hear her. When my car came to a stop she passed again through the front end of my car and entered the church. There was a bright flash of light and everything was quiet. I have no idea who she was or what had happened to her, and I really don't care. I helped someone find peace that night, and Jon got to see what being a ghost is really like.

I've crossed several others over, but the stories are largely inconsequential. The encounters amounted to me just saying "you're dead crossover" and that's about it.

During this time of me crossing ghosts over and not going to church I was still part of the Church in that I still had my name on the membership roster. So as my beliefs began to change, and I started to form my own opinions I was committing heresy.

Just so there is no confusion: heresy is the going against what the Church or religious governing body says about whatever issue they happen have codified. For example saying that the Messiah has come and was named Jesus is heresy to Jews; saying the opposite is heresy to Christians. Heresy is nothing more than a difference of opinion or belief; blasphemy which is often confused with heresy is going against the laws of God such as saying "God dammit"; that's the fourth commandment for anyone keeping track.

Now according to the Mormon Church I have committed heresy especially during this time in my life. The things that I did were for the most part quite minor, but it was all of them stacked together that made me get into the trouble that I did. One of the biggest reasons that I broke from the Church was the fact that I am psychic and in the Church no one other than the Prophet and his inner circle is allowed to be psychic by any means. They can be the only ones with a direct link to God; otherwise chaos will ensue because the people will begin to form their own opinions about divinity. That would destabilize the Church and cause civil wars over ideology. So being psychic is heavily discouraged and even hunted down more fervently than is homosexuality. So for most of my life I lived in hiding in plain sight until I broke from the Church. As a result of my leaving, I declared war.

This was more of a Jihad than a war however. I wanted to destroy and take vengeance upon the Church for the lies that they had told me and the pain that I had felt and for all the other people that they were conning. But it wasn't just the Mormon Church that I wanted to destroy—I wanted to destroy them all. Mormon, Catholic, Lutheran, Jew, Muslim, Buddhist, etc.; any form of organized religion as far as I was concerned existed only for the personal gain of the clergy and the enslavement of the parishioners. I started to think about how I could do it; it would be a big task and I would need help. Then one night while I was meditating I had a vision.

I will warn you that this is one thing that I will not edit for sensitive sensibilities. If you do not like course language, you might want to skip the next paragraph.

My guide James was sitting in front of me with his legs crossed, he looked upset. I thought that he had come before me to give me some ideas about how I could start bringing down the Churches. This is what he said to me: "Who the fuck do you think you are? How dare you think that you know more than All Mighty God?! Did you not think that we have religion in place for a reason, and if we did not want it that it would be wiped away just as quickly?! Those institutions exist for the help of humanity. They are there to help people who are not strong to be good and not an animal. If you think you can go at this world alone without any human help, that's fine. If you think you can understand God and do everything you need to do by yourself, be our guest. But please afford the same right to everyone around you. Let them make their own mistakes. Let them learn on their own time and in their own way. Otherwise you are no better than the perceived despots you are trying to overthrow."

I suddenly fell out of meditation. I sat for a moment and reflected on what I had just been told. I started to weep, and I begged for forgiveness. The war was over before it had begun.

I know I say a lot of bad things about the Mormon Church. Each one of those things is only true when applied to certain individuals, not to the organization itself. Saying that the entire Church is evil because of a few racists is like saying that everybody who speaks German is an anti-Semitic Nazi because that's what Hitler was. Or that all Italians are in the

Mafia because the Italian Mob is the most high profile. These ideas are ludicrous. While I do not like organized religion, I do support it if it gets you closer to God and gives you a reason to get up in the morning. However, if the religion does things that you do not like or has policies that you do not agree with, then you should probably reconsider your membership.

Vairin had been kicked out of his place for dating his Latina girlfriend, so Jon invited him to stay at the house that I told you about in Downtown Salt Lake. His parents had just bought the place and were moving in. Vairin had just gotten home from working the night shift so he lied down for a nap. A short time later, he woke up and started playing with his guitar. He was startled by the sound of footsteps coming up from the basement. He thought it was Jon getting home from school so Vairin called after him. No answer. The footsteps were now in the kitchen. Vairin called for Jon again. No answer. Vairin put is guitar down and walked out of his room to find who was making the noise. He found no one, but he continued to hear the footsteps which were now in the master bedroom. So Vairin grabbed an old sword that Jon's dad had received from the navy, and he started to clear the house. He found no one. Then he heard the back door open and more footsteps in the kitchen. He turned to see Scott standing there, and as Scott says, "I saw Vairin standing there with a sword in his underwear." What Scott meant was, "Vairin was standing there in his underwear holding a sword." The guys did suspect the house as being haunted so they took it upon themselves to have the place blessed and get rid of the ghost.

About a year after I left the Church I graduated from college and began massage school. One of my teachers was this hippie-type guy named C. B. He was awesome. As a kid he was very dangerous, more so than I was. Now he had an air of calmness and peace and joy around him that I found just intoxicating. He taught me some Tai Qi and some Qi Gong and how to meditate properly. Up until that time I had been meditating very shallowly and for only a couple of minutes at a time. He showed me what I was doing wrong, and he did it in a single day.

We were meditating in class and I said in my own mind that there was a lot of pain in the room; then I realized it was coming from me. I decided to go deeper and chase the pain instead of running from it like I had done all my life. I followed the sensation down through my body and through each of my chakras. From the crown of my head to the one in my belly were just fine; in the lowest one I found something. It was so horrible I had a full anxiety attack. C. B. scooted closer to me at the end of class to see if I was okay. I wasn't. He talked through what to do to beat this thing and actually advised me to eat the biggest ugliest hamburger I could find to settle my mind. I was very embarrassed for allowing my emotions to run around like that. After all I had been taught all my life that men aren't supposed to show or even have emotion.

So for the next 2 years under the tutelage of C. B., I set out to cleanse myself of these horrible emotions that were gumming up my chakras. I appeared to be successful. I was happy finally. My abilities were great. I could read easily. I could heal easily. Even my tarot readings were on the money. My mind was clear, and I could use my emotions as I felt necessary. I was in complete control.

Soon afterward I moved to California. Something wonderful and at the same time horrible happened that changed everything.

PREACHERS, SAGES AND FOOLS

My formal education began in the fall of 1989 with my entry into kindergarten at Edgemont Elementary, but I was already very well educated before that. According to my mom, I had zero interest in nursery rhymes. She and my dad read to me every single day at least one book, we averaged about three. I'm sure you can guess this got old pretty fast especially since I had favorites that loved to have read to me.

As a kid I would not sleep unless I had my reading and I was sufficiently exhausted. So my mom got creative; she read me encyclopedias. For those of you that came into this world after the creation of the internet, when us "old people" were young we had these things called encyclopedias that were books indexed alphabetically and came in a set of about 10 to 20 books. This library held information for just about everything you could ever want to know about. The actual library, that is to say the building where they keep all those books was still in use back then; and when you wanted to know about something you went there and got a book.

This tactic of reading some of the most boring literature that my mom could find to get me to sleep was at first very effective. At least she got some sleep. We had this book about predatory mammals like big cats that I just loved. We would start reading it and my mom would pass out from boredom; I would stay awake and thumb through it and look at all the pictures (I was 4 and couldn't read yet) of the animals like lions, weasels, wolves and so many others. Because of my mom, when I entered kindergarten I knew more about the difference between a lynx and a bobcat than I did about some dish and a spoon.

My entertainment was for the most part thanks to public television. I watched everything from Sesame Street to Mr. Rodgers. I even named my cat after one of the characters. I did watch regular cartoons like GI Joe and Bugs Bunny, but those were largely set aside for Saturday mornings.

I was really sensitive as a kid, and I was always getting into trouble. I seriously thought that until I was about 5 that my name was Ricky-god-dammit. And it was because that as a kid I was always in trouble that I hated the holidays. I would get too excited and start running around and I would get yelled at for being noisy. I was to be a good little boy and just sit there and play with my trucks and not bother the grown-ups. I did not start to like the holidays until I was about ten. Christmas I loved because I never got in trouble then, but the other ones I just hated. People please let your kids play and be kids. They have the rest of their lives to be miserable, at least give them as much joy in their childhood as you can. Don't coddle them, but not be harsh with them either.

When I entered kindergarten I was the smartest kid in the class, which made me a nerd. I was the first in the class the count to 100 and to learn how to read and write. Half the kids hadn't even been potty trained yet, and I was tying my own shoes. According to my mom the first report I ever gave was in kindergarten about how an airplane flies, and I was right. Everyone including my teacher was mystified. I had done well, and my parents were proud of me.

The next report I gave was about what I wanted to be when I grew up. It was an entire day at school, and we had to dress up. There was a doctor and a house wife and an astronaut—the regular kid stuff. I wanted to be a paleontologist, and I dressed the part. I knew what it was, it was somebody that dug in the dirt, which was something that I loved to do anyway, and find dinosaur bones. I think what my teacher was really amazed about was that I knew what a paleontologist was and that I could even say the word.

The next year something happened to me that sowed the seeds of issues that I would face for the rest of my life. I had the opportunity to take the first standardized test of my life. It took about 20 minutes for the teacher to explain what we were doing and why we were doing it. We were given a pencil, a piece of paper with a bunch of circles and numbers and letters on it, a booklet and a small cubicle looking thing called an "office". We were instructed that we had a limited amount of time, but not to rush and to just do our best. When we were allowed to begin I opened my booklet and started answering questions. I was among the first to finish. My teacher came over to me, took my test away and told me to find something to do. So I worked on my art stuff and waited for the other kids to finish. After everything was collected we went back to class and everything was fine.

About 2 weeks later I was called into the principal's office. When I got down there my dad was waiting for me along with the principal. I was taken into the principal's office without my dad and asked if I remembered taking the big test a couple of weeks ago. I said I did. Then he asked if I had looked on anybody else's paper. I said no, I couldn't the offices were in the way. He then asked if I knew that I not only did the best in the class but I was one of the smartest kids in the country. I had no idea what he was talking about.

I had been pulled into the principal's office because I had done too well on a test. They thought that I had cheated. I suspect now that it was racially or gender-bias motivated, but that cannot be proven. That meeting caused a glitch inside of me that would stay with me until I started writing this book.

This seed was fostered the following year by a horrible teacher. At the start of every year my mom and I would go to the school and see who my teacher was and who was in my class. For second grade I had Mrs. J. We found her room and went to go meet her. We approached the classroom and looked in to see if she was there, she wasn't. I said to my mom that I didn't want to be there, and that I didn't want her as my teacher. But my mom didn't listen to me and said she told me not to worry that this was a nice teacher; she had teddy bears on the wall.

The following week the year started off. I had a great day. I got to see all my friends again, I was happy. A few weeks later we started something that my teacher called the timed test. We were in second grade and starting to learn multiplication. So as a test of our skill and to prove that we were doing our homework we were given a sheet of paper with 20 or 30 simple multiplication problems on it. One minute was placed on the clock, and we had to answer as many of them as we possibly could in that time. After the test we traded with a neighbor and corrected the test. The smart kids on a good day got around ten to fifteen. The not so smart kids averaged about eight. On a good day I was one of the smart kids and on a bad day I was one of the not so smart kids.

My teacher was livid with the class and the results of the test. We took the test every day. And every day she would slam the door shut and yell at us for about 20 minutes. She would tell us that we were stupid, that we were nothing compared to her kids in the fourth grade who could do the whole thing in less than a minute, that we would never amount to anything if we couldn't do this, and that we should never tell our mommies and daddies about what she was saying to us. Children in the class would cry in the classroom, and she would yell at them specifically telling them to shut up or she would give them something to cry about.

After about 7 months of this abuse the damage had been done to me and many members of my class; I at least had now made the assumption that I was stupid. But instead of falling back and letting myself get pushed around I fought back the only way I knew how: I became smarter. I decided to prove to everyone around me and to myself that Mrs. J. was wrong, and that I was smart. I decided that I would never be accused of cheating again, that I would be cheated off of because I would know everything.

During all of my elementary school education we were taught and re-taught how to read. The system that was used was called "Open Court". When people are taught how to read usually they are told what each of the characters sounds like and then the sounds are put together to form a word. If that word is known and all of the other words are known then the sentence makes sense, and the written message is conveyed to the reader. That is not how I was taught to read in school.

We were instead told a story that specified the sounds of the sounds of the letters rather than the letters themselves. Within this story there was a character or event surrounding the sound of a given letter or group of letters. For example, for R we had "Roaring Lion" because lions when they roar go RRRRRR, or something. The emphasis was on phonics, but there is a problem with that: unless where you live speaks English perfectly words will get muddled together and then you can't spell or communicate properly. This system only works if the accent of the people using the system is not deviant from Standard English. Utahn is very deviant; not as bad as some of the Southern accents, but the point remains. My mom actually taught me how to read in the traditional form, and I just made it look like I was using their system.

Earlier I wrote about not liking to sing or play music. I had some bad experiences in school regarding this subject. This was the issue. Every 1 to 2 days the entire grade would be herded into a classroom and ordered to sing various songs. They were always season appropriate and always just for kids. They tended to be kind of old however. We sang nothing from the 1960's or later. Until I was in middle school I actually thought that nobody had written music since the time of the Beatles. We had to sing every song. If we did not want to sing a given song we got sent to the principal's office, and likely suspended. That's a good idea, scare small children into having fun.

I studied and read and watched PBS until my tiny kid brain was numb. I soaked up every bit of knowledge I could find. When the other kids were out playing, I was learning. Then in third grade I had a teacher that called me a scientist. He fostered it and tried to build it. The trouble was he was old and crazy. It kind of killed his credibility.

Fourth grade was even better. As I wrote earlier I was cool that year, and my teacher helped with that. Then one day I had an issue in class and someone called me stupid. I ran out of the classroom and disappeared to the far end of the playground where I knew my teacher wouldn't look for me. Had I known what that was the start of, I never would have done it.

There was one awesome time in fourth grade though that I do remember. It was the fourth grade kick ball tournament. We were called the Braves. We had 2 of the grade's top athletes on our team and we all got along relatively well. There was only one other team that even came close to us; they had the other top athlete and they gave us a run for our money. I think they were the Yankees, but I'm not sure. Our 2 teams traded first and second spots all throughout the season, with the championship game coming down to us. The game was tight. I honestly did not know who was going to win, but with one final kick the Braves won it!

The next 2 years of school were really bad. The first part of fifth grade seemed to go well with my hosting of a star party in my back yard. A star party is an evening where people get together drink hot apple cider—virgin of course we're kids—and look at stars and planets through a telescope. The party was a hit, but I learned something soon afterward. I learned that in order to gain and keep friends I had to keep buying their affection with parties and gifts. This is a lesson that until recently I upheld as a basic law of the universe with no exception.

During fifth grade I was a complete nerd and a total loser. I had horrible hygiene and I was starting puberty. My voice was actually cracking at the end of fourth grade and I had peach fuzz thick enough to shave by the middle of fifth grade. Suffice it to say I didn't have much of a social life.

There was an exception to this though: one day in the middle of April during recess it started to rain. We were all out playing basketball, I of course sucked but that wasn't important I was having fun. We were called in because it is illegal for the school to have children out in the rain in Utah. Everybody went inside except for the few of us playing the game. Somebody decided that we should change the rules and play "jungle ball". This is a variation on basketball. Basically, the rules concerning fouls are thrown out, and just about anything goes as long as there is no blood and no broken bones. Playing this in the rain was a blast. We must have been out there for 30 or 40 minutes. When we finally finished we went back inside soaked and sore. We all expected to go to the principal's office, but none of the teachers seemed to care.

I continued to study constantly and maintain my standing in the near if not top of my class throughout the nation. The price of this was my sanity.

When sixth grade rolled around something odd happened. A class had been created that included all of the smart kids; it was called the gifted class. The odd thing was I wasn't in it. I had a genius IQ, and I was placed in a class with the regular and dumb kids. I could only think of one thing…I was actually stupid. My teacher was very pregnant and gave birth sometime in November. I told my mom what was going on, and she said she would look into it. The school got back to us in January. I was not placed in that class due to a lack of intelligence or poor test scores, quite the opposite was true. I had been placed in the class as a student teacher without my knowledge or consent. My job according to the school board was to teach the regular kids and make them as smart as me.

As I said, in November my teacher had a baby and left her class for 5 months. During this time we got a long-term substitute teacher that did not know who or what I was doing in her class. I was told to teach the other kids, but I couldn't relate to them and I was being treated like one of them. This was causing me to misinterpret how I related to the world and translated into a very prominent mental disorder. One day in class during a particularly bad day, one of the kids called me "fat". I got so angry that I blacked out. I apparently lunged over the desk and tackled the kid; I wrapped my arm around his neck and started to choke him to death. I woke up when the teacher pulled me off of him. I looked at the kid's face as he got up from me; he was coughing and his face was purple. I went to the principal's office and told him what had happened. No harm came to me and the kid that I had tackled never messed with me again.

I became increasingly withdrawn, and I refused to take part in any form of playing especially at recess. When I was asked what my favorite anything was, my reply was, "I have no favorites." I got into fights almost daily. In one instance a kid actually shoved a pine cone in my eye. The school did nothing for 3 hours with the exception of giving me ice. They did finally decide to call my dad and I got released to go to the hospital, but nothing happened to the kid that injured me. The school said that I had deserved it, and that my assailant was defending himself. I had to wear a patch on my right eye for about a week while I healed. There was a minor legal battle with the kid's family, but nothing ever came of it. Even though I was the one always being attacked, I was the one that always got in trouble. My parents tried to get me transferred to another school, but the school board wouldn't approve my visa to go a couple of blocks down the street. They just told me to "suck it up and stop being a girl".

My graduation from grade school to middle school was a godsend. Recess was gone. Ninety percent of all the people that had messed with me were gone. I also didn't have to spend all day with the same teacher and the same people. This was my chance to start again, and get away from my past. It was a resounding success.

Mount Jordan Middle School was so much better than Edgemont Elementary that I may as well had moved to a new city. For the most part my teachers were halfway decent, only 1 or 2 were idiots and spouting non-factual information like the American Indians worshipped Jesus before the arrival of Europeans and that no actual scientist believes that humans came from apes. These things are of course religious doctrine, and they have no place in a public school no matter what religion's doctrine they might be part of.

It was in middle school that I learned what it was like to actually be included in a society no matter how small it may be. This is of course in relation to my friends such as Scott and Vairin and the group that I became part of. The main catalyst for our group was Drama Club. Because of the hell that I went through in grade school I was a perfect candidate to become an actor, and I was good at it or at least I thought I was.

We had a great time in the club, which was headed up by our English teacher that we affectionately called "Harvey Wallbanger". I have no idea to this day why we called him that. I do remember the first day of class; Harvey came out of the closet. Before class in my eighth grade year, he had stashed himself in the room's coat closet and then he exited the closet a few seconds after the bell to the stunned amusement of the entire class. Harvey was our patron, and he attended some of our parties. He is the one that wrote *WordRumble* and the director of the *Diary of Anne Frank.* At best with me I was always in a supporting role, while Scott and Vairin were in leading roles. I was actually fine with it, because they were my friends and we all can't have the lead. I was actually a terrible actor, but I wouldn't figure that out for several more years.

One of the greatest things that ever happened at my school was the fruition of a stupid human joke. The joke is you tell someone that gullible is written on the ceiling. They look, and you laugh at them for being dumb and the day goes on. One of the kids in my class, we called him "Grandma" due to a picture that we took of him during the *Diary of Anne Frank*, he actually wrote "gullible" in green dry erase marker on the ceiling of the drama room but he spelled it "guilable". To the best of my knowledge it is still there, and we are the only people that know who put it there.

During middle school I continued to study and excel, and I maintained my status in the near top of the nation academically. For once in my life this was a good thing. I got into classes that actually stimulated me and challenged me. I did however learn something about math after my accident with the car and the bike. I have to sleep in a math class. If I am awake during a math class, I cannot learn it; but if I sleep I can wake up, do the day's work hand it in, ace it, and then pass the test and class with minimal study time. I don't understand why it works, but it does and it held true from ninth grade to college when I took statistics.

I loved middle school for the most part. I had friends. My classes were easy, but challenging at the same time. I had purpose in my life. When it came time for high school I wanted to ensure that this never left me. There were some issues and bumps that I have already talked about, but everything seemed so easy. I made the decision to create my empire at Jordan High with B. G. as my second.

Jordan High was one of the first high schools in the Salt Lake Valley. It was established in 1907 in a small home of the only teacher in the school, and it finally got a building in 1914. This was called "Old

Jordan" in 1996 when the "New Jordan" building was built as a result of dilapidation. The grounds of the old building have since been turned into an office building, 4 restaurants and a 17 theater megaplex. The institution of the school has a storied past. Railroad tracks run behind the grounds of both the old and new buildings, and it was on these tracks that a stalled bus carrying the 1938 Jordan High football team was hit by a freight train. This of course led to rumors of ghosts out on the football field and gym and theatre. Based on firsthand experience and accounts from several teachers and students, I would say that there is substance to these rumors.

The school has many traditions including one that every member of the student council has participated in for the last hundred-some-odd years. At the time of inauguration, every member lops the top off of a giant sugar beet and takes a bite. The reason for this is Jordan High of Sandy, Utah is the home of the Beetdiggers. A beetdigger is actually a large knife verging on sword with a big flat hook on the business end; this is a tool used by the beet farmers that used to populate Sandy before it was incorporated. Many of the students in the original classes were the children of these farmers. Thus the school mascot is a big ugly farmer wielding a big sword looking thing and pulling a big sugar beet out of the ground.

My sophomore year was awesome. I had a great history teacher that made learning fun by playing music as we walked into class that was relevant to the day's lesson. She also spoke to us like we were adults. This was my favorite teacher of the year.

I also learned how to drive; and yes I was terrible. I had this driver's ed teacher that was a real jerk. He would give me directions that were not specific and then he would get mad at me for not being able to follow what he said. He called me a stoner one day—I do not, have never, and will never smoke anything—and I yelled back at him. I learned to drive despite my education, and my dad and mom and brother-in-law were instrumental in that. With the exceptions of running over a neighborhood watch sign thanks to an icy road, not paying attention at a stop sign, accidentally rear-ending somebody that had stopped short, and turning because somebody told me to turn when I should have waited…I'm a fantastic driver now.

When I was learning how to drive, I asked my brother-in-law to teach me how to drive stick. He agreed. So we borrowed my mom's car and took it out for a spin. I had never been so scared in my life. He eventually figured out that I was having a really hard time and we went home, but in the course of that I almost got into a big accident because Utah drivers don't pay attention to what is in front of them. When we got home I leapt out of the car and rushed to my room where I sat and trembled like I had malaria. I have not tried to drive a stick since.

My very first accident was the slipping on an icy road and running over a neighborhood watch sign. I got a ticket because a cop just happened to be passing by. I of course fought the ticket and lost. The presiding judge told me that if I ever fought another ticket again she would personally see that I went to jail. So now I have a mild distrust of legal authority. This was finally resolved when I realized that cops are just people trying to get by and working a very dangerous job.

My next accident occurred a few months later when I ran a stop sign and nicked the front of another car. No injuries, minor damage. The third accident happened during my junior year on The Witch's birthday. My car was totaled but my dad rebuilt it. Then my senior year, I rear-ended somebody that stopped short and I had to get a new bumper again. See not so bad, and that is all that has happened.

During my sophomore year I decided to join the school wrestling team. My brother-in-law was a former wrestler and football player for Jordan; in fact he had met and dated my older sister because they had gone to school together. More on her later. My brother-in-law had tried to teach me to be a sports guy like him since we met. He attempted to take a scared little wuss and turn him into a manly-man. All previous attempts with baseball had failed; I just wasn't good at it and I tended to over-think. So in order to make him proud of me and me proud of myself I joined the wrestling team with Vairin.

This was a mistake. The coach was an idiot. He starved us, and forbade us from drinking water so that we could keep a low weight. We did high level cardio every practice and only worked on basic moves which focused only on defense.

I actually remember leaving practice one night with my back pack and walking outside to where this nice lady with long brown hair was waiting for me in a tiny blue car. I stood there smiling at her like a fool. She told me to get in the car, I did and we drove off. I had no idea where I was going, but when we got there, she led me into a house and sat me down on a couch. She then went behind a wall into a kitchen and started preparing food. There were these 2 furry creatures walking around that seemed to know me. I asked what they were, and I was told by the nice lady that they were my cats. I was given a plate of food a few minutes later. The meal consisted of a pork chop, broccoli and pasta. I got angry with the lady and said that my coach told me I wasn't allowed to eat pasta because it would make me fat. I was assured that I would be fine and I should eat it.

A few bites into the meal I realized where I was and who this nice lady was; I was at home and she was my mother. I was so malnourished that I didn't know what anything was. My mom asked me what I was eating during the day, and I told her that we were only allowed to have protein and a few vegetables with no fruit or carbohydrates of any form. We were not allowed to have any water especially during practice. The logic is the human body is mostly water, so to drop weight you just stop drinking water. That makes about as much sense as saying to save money on the space program cut out oxygen. Wrestlers want to be at a low weight so they have more agility, and in theory, more flexibility. The problem comes when vital nutrients like say sugar, which runs our cells, is cut out and the body has to eat itself to function. Of course weight is going to drop and along with it strength, flexibility, speed and intelligence. It shouldn't be a surprise that Jordan has never won a wrestling tournament to the best of my knowledge.

After that episode, I quit the team the following week. I handed my singlet and head gear over to my coach as he passed by in the hall. I was free.

One of the things that did bother me about school in Utah was this: we were not allowed to read. That's not entirely true. We had access to all the books of the world, but we could not read them because we had too much other stuff to read. The other stuff was the same stuff year end and out. For example I read the *Odyssey* 3 times, the *Great Gatsby* 3 times and *Great Expectations* twice. All the books that we read once were books that I had never heard of. The worst one of these that sticks out in my mind is *Cold Sassy Tree*. It's about a young boy in the Deep South with a physically and mentally damaged uncle and a teacher that he and his uncle both have a crush on. It was terrible. I asked my teacher about this and she said it was an American classic. American classic my hairy you-know-what; it was a dime store novel, and it read like one. This nonsense plagued me all through my secondary education and especially in high school. We were given such crap to read, and we often only had the weekend to do it in. I don't remember many of the books because I had to blow through them and take a test on the entire two to four hundred pages the following week.

I did not get to read any real classics like *Frankenstein, Dracula, A Tale of Two Cities, Sherlock Holmes, Canterbury Tales, Paradise Lost, The Divine Comedy, The Count of Monte Cristo,* etc. unless I read them of my own accord. I read *The Count of Monte Cristo* my sophomore year for history class, and loved it. I read *Frankenstein* by myself my senior year for a summer English project—loved it. I picked up *The Prince, The Art of War* and *The Art of Peace* that year as well and they formed the basis for much of philosophical process during my adult life.

The only respite we got from this censorship was in my senior year AP English class. My teacher who was new to Salt Lake City from the East Coast loved the classics and wanted us to read them, so she gave us the option for the summer before class to read one of several books from the American Classics list; I picked *Frankenstein.* I asked her why several other books were not on the list, and she said that they were banned by the state school board because they were too risqué for young readers. You see, apparently ultra-conservative Victorian literature is just too nasty for the new saints of God. It was because of this teacher, who shall go nameless, that I realized if I wanted to learn about the world and survive in it after high school I had take to matters into my own hands and not rely on my education. Nothing new here.

As I have said several times, I don't remember a lot my junior year. I do remember taking AP Biology and almost failing the organic chemistry section. I got a 4 out of 5 on the year end test and qualified for college credit. I remember bits and pieces of AP US History and that I loved the class. I got a 3 out of 5 on that test and also got college credit. I remember flashes of auto shop and a few other classes that can't remember the names of. I do remember that I hated my Honors English teacher though.

There was no love lost between us. She was a know-it-all, and respected no one. There was one kid in the class that she liked. He was just like her—a total jerk. She gave us stories to read and told us to interpret what the author was getting at; we were of course wrong. She would tell us that to our faces and then tell us what the "correct" answer was. I am not one to be pushed around. I spent a lot of my life being pushed around and I do not take it. When we read a story called *The Bear* we were asked what the bear in the story symbolized, she just told us that the bear symbolized truth. I asked why, and she yelled at me in class and then kicked me out. That was actually the third time she did it. The first was during the reading of a short story by Herman Melville, the author of *Moby Dick.* The story featured a sailor that didn't fit in well with his crewmates. He didn't understand how they behaved and seemed to act strangely around them. She said that this sailor was a Christ-like figure because he didn't fit in well and was essentially innocent. I called her on it. I said, "How is that possible? He exhibits no Christ qualities like non-violence and understanding of humanity. Just because he is innocent does not mean that he is divine. He is nothing like Jesus." She ordered me out into the hall. When we got out there she stuck her bony finger in my chest and told me that if I ever contradicted her in class again she would have me kicked out of school.

From then on everything that I said in class was wrong, except for on rare occasions when I was right, and I would say, "Wow I was right, better mark that on the calendar." Then she sent me out into the hall again. She would tell us to write essays about what we were reading, and then yell at us for the remainder of class because we didn't know how to write essays without using the word "I". In the Utah AP and Honors level classes, students are not supposed to have any opinions, we are just supposed to regurgitate information and honor "teachers" that died decades before and use their lines of logic even if they are completely wrong.

So I decided to rebel against this. I started writing short stories that all had one thing in common: they all had a character named "Tom". I picked that name because of the apostle Thomas who doubted things. In every story "Tom" was described differently and held a different role in the plot. My goal was to have the book of stories published and wind up in English classes all over the country, and laugh at all the teachers trying to make sense out of why "Tom" is so pervasive when there is no symbolic intention other than I'm screwing with you. You see, sometimes something in a story has no hidden meaning (well most of the time) and it's just there. I have noticed with a lot of English teachers they read into what they're reading and come up with some really outlandish stuff. Those stories have since been destroyed because they sucked. Sorry to disappoint you.

Another small thing that I remember is the junior talent show. I was part of it, and I was in a sword fight on stage with my friend and fellow actor S. T. We had known each other since grade school and he was one of the few people that treated me like person during my spell of insanity as a kid. S. T. was a total dork, and a big drama geek. He and I had a lot of fun choreographing that fight, from what I remember that is. S. T. would go on to play the Scarecrow in the *Wizard of Oz* at the school and hold several other high profile parts all throughout high school.

Another small thing that I remember was my pre-calculus class. The reason for this was my teacher. She was about 25, gorgeous and brilliant. She stood about as tall as me in heals, had long blonde hair and a great smile. I was in lust at first sight. I'm not proud of it but I actually had a sex dream about her in class while I was sleeping, like I do in all my math classes. About halfway through the year she got married to a statistician named Melvin and moved away. All the guys in the class were heartbroken. I think I dropped the class soon after, but I don't remember. She was and is the only teacher that I have ever had a crush on.

My senior year was a lot better and I remember most of it. I took this class called "American Problems", which was a basic polisci class. In this class we didn't really have lectures we instead got to experience different issues within the political arena. We were placed in a police state. I got to run for president. We held a mock trial on racism and free speech. We even had a model UN. And yes I am going into specifics.

With the police state project, for 2 or 3 weeks we pretended that our nation had been the victim of a coup and had turned totalitarian. We were not allowed to smile or to call each other by name only by number. I was chosen to be the leader of the secret police and ordered to root out all dissidents. I performed my job admirably. I used my training as an actor and became the part. I secretly wanted to overthrow the chairman and institute my own regime, but we didn't have the time. I did however become a magistrate towards the end. My teacher even told me at the end that I had scared him with how ruthless I was. In all actuality I was just playing a part in a play.

Next we turned the class room into the US Senate. I represented the Carolinas, and I actually chose to create a different personality for either state. For example I had a joke with South Carolina saying, "The South shall rise again," and North Carolina saying, "Shut up they ain't supposed to know that yet." I don't think many people got it. You see, it's funny because South Carolina was the first state to secede during the American Civil War. Anyway, near the end of the simulation we had a presidential election. I got together with B. G. and another of my friends and we all decided to run. B. G. backed out of the race and I was the only one that survived the primaries. I went up against the smart jock in the class. He was a huge jerk and we did not get along at all. I almost beat him but I lost by only 5 electoral votes.

In the mock trial, we used the actual case involving a Nazi protest of a Jewish Synagogue in the 1970's which resulted in a riot. I played the part of the Jewish ACLU lawyer chosen to defend the leader of the Nazi protesters. I kicked ass. I managed to get the bastard acquitted of a few of the charges, but he still went to jail for inciting a riot. The point of the exercise was to get us to think about other people besides ourselves and the whole point of free speech.

The model UN was fun. We were given a map of the world and each student was chosen to represent a given political power in the world. These included: USA, UK, Spain, Italy, Greece, Iran, China, Israel, Palestinians, Egypt, Japan, Syria, Mexico, and then Iraq played by me. Come to think of it I think my teacher liked screwing with me. Anyway, I played Iraq during the invasion of it by the US and her allies. I was trying to work behind the scenes to unify the Middle East against Western Imperialists. One of my friends was playing the part of Al Qaida and I had a not-so-secret arrangement with him that when questioned about it I denied. Then NATO attacked me led by the US. The first volley was the assassination of Saddam Hussein; I declared war, and I lost against the allied attack. As a result I became a liberation front entity and started picking off parts of the nations that had attacked me. In the simulation I kidnapped the Pope, cut off his ring finger and sent it to the White House with a note that said, "Get out of my country." They did not listen so I bombed the Golden Gate Bridge and the Athenian Acropolis. I kept doing things like this every turn, hoping they would get the point. Of course the kids in the class didn't. Every single rogue nation that they attacked and conquered became a friend of mine and we started to really chip at the US and NATO. I did get bored eventually with the attacking of only the US. So I attacked China. I anthraxed a bunch of rice fields just before the kid declared a rice festival. I laughed so hard I hyperventilated. On the last day of the simulation the US did finally leave, and I renounced terrorism.

Best class project ever!

If your high school has anything like this class, please take it. It will be the highlight of your senior year.

For the most part the major thing in my senior year was drama club. We produced a play by Neil Simon called *Rumors*. I auditioned, but didn't land any parts. So

I became the props manager. This was actually very fun. I got to hang out with my friends like Scott and watch rehearsals every day. I actually memorized the entire play for about a year afterward, because I had heard it so much. Even thought I wasn't part of the cast, I was part of the crew and I treasure that time.

Another play we did was *1984*. I auditioned for O'Brian, but got the Loud Speaker part and Guard instead. I worked them. I was determined to be the best I could be. And in the reviews of the school paper, I was one of the scariest parts of the play as the Loud Speaker. I loved that review because I wanted people to fear me. I had been conditioned that I couldn't be loved so I should be feared and thus respected. Man, was I wrong. I also realized as we did the play, that there were a lot of similarities to that world and the city in which I lived. I formed a very logical belief that I was living in a totalitarian state. It made sense to me: only one entity controlled media and education and commerce. This belief however true or false it may have actually been made me very depressed and a little paranoid.

One of the best parts of the play was a mistake that the lead made. He was supposed to say that, "…freedom is the ability to say that two plus two equals four." What he actually said was, "…two plus two equals five—four!" Scott and I had to run outside so we wouldn't get caught laughing backstage. During my performance as a guard I had to be hard and emotionless, as did everyone else including Scott. I imagined that if we were in a sitcom and the camera panned over us and entered our thoughts everyone including Scott would be thinking, "I'm evil. I have no soul. I have no emotion.

Grrr." And then when the camera got to me, "Gum drops lollypops and rainbows everywhere. I'm so happy." When I told this joke at the cast party, it killed.

One of the most fun plays that I got to be part of was for Shakespeare class. We put on *The Merry Wives of Windsor*. I was one of the directors, and a Page. Scott was Falstaff, and hilarious. We had a blast with this play. One of the highlights was me acting confused as to what had just happened during a reversal of the obvious plot line and then skipping off stage. We again got rave reviews, and cemented our place in the pantheon of Jordan High drama gods.

After about the middle of my third quarter of senior year I kind of blacked out. From about the middle of March to graduation day everything is a fuzzy blur with a few pockets of clarity. The reason for this was I should have graduated early, but I was young and stupid and I wanted to be part of the plays that we were producing, specifically *1984.* I also wanted to go to the senior prom. All these things were only open to students so I chose to stay on. I should not have done that. Kids, if you have the chance to get out of high school and start college early, please take it; don't stick around for stupid high school crap.

One of the things that I do remember was the Senior Awards Assembly which was held for high ranking students in the senior class and their parents. Because of my excellent academics I was invited. I got the program when we entered the auditorium, and my name was on the credits. I thought this was cool. That impression changed. The entire assembly turned into just a foray for the football elites and their contributions to the school. This made no sense to me. First of all, the team had failed to win hardly any of their games during the season much less make it to State, so we knew most of the players sucked. Second, I was worlds above them in academics and extra-curriculars. I was livid by the time the assembly was over and I was not called. My parents and I stormed out without saying a word to anyone.

I left Jordan behind me June of 2002. I was very happy to be gone. Graduation day rolled around, and we all went to the expo center next door to the school for the ceremony. Why was it not at the school, I don't know, Utah is weird. Even though I was leaving Jordan High with less than stellar memories, the school still had 2 more tricks up its sleeve for me. The first was we were not allowed to throw our hats at the end of the ceremony. I did not know this because no one had told me. I threw my hat, and got into a lot of trouble. The way the attending faculty looked at me you would have thought I had just committed mass murder. The second technically happened before the hat thing. When you get your diploma you get a picture of the event for your parents. My picture got mixed up with another kid's and we did not find out about it until July when it arrived in our mailbox. In the defense of the photographer, the other guy and I did look alike. We both had tan skin and dark hair and looked the same from the back, but from the front it is obvious; the other guy was Mexican—I actually knew him—where I am clearly not. Jackasses.

I started at Westminster College in Salt Lake City the following September. I felt like I had been released from prison. I was urged to ask questions, and to have an opinion. It was great.

For those of you who do not know about Westminster, I will explain. The school itself was founded in the mid-19th century by a Presbyterian minister, but is now nondenominational and private and liberal ed. The entire campus is only 2 blocks from north to south and one block from east to west. The entire student body including undergrad and graduate levels numbers only about 2500. The school is tiny and very expensive. I'm sure you're wondering how I got in when I'm poor. The answer is my grades. Among the schools that I applied to, Westminster gave me the most money. Its sister school, Northwestern in Washington gave me nothing, not even a rejection letter. The University of Utah gave me a pittance of a thousand dollars. Westminster gave me a big scholarship totaling to about one quarter of my tuition. Yeah, I went to Westminster.

Even though I was the first male in my family to attend a 4 year institution, I was still a legacy. My sister had attended Westminster 10 years before me, and was also a big reason for my entry.

I was surprised to hear that there were no Greek organizations at the school. There are no frats and no sororities at Westminster. The reason being the school is too small, and if the school did have Greeks the resulting turf wars would likely tear the school and surrounding community apart. As a result the school is very close knit. There are parties and lectures and events that are always going on at Westminster, and I took part in several of them.

The first thing that happened to me with Westminster was the Freshman Campout. I had grown up in a very quiet part of Salt Lake; even the rowdy kids were in bed by midnight. The party went until 2 AM. But that night I got to go on stage and do some stand-up. I killed. I asked how many people were coming in from out of town. Several cheers. I said that they have probably discovered that Utahns don't talk like the rest of the country. For example Utahns say, "oh my heck." This is because Utahns don't like to swear, and heck is a word used by children and people from Utah. That joke alone held the crowd. The next day, I went on a big hike and ended up holding up the entire bus train. Sorry about that.

My English comp. professor told me that using the word "I" was a good thing. We were taught that our opinions were valid, and that we should completely forget about everything that we had learned in high school about writing and understanding what we were reading. I loved her and aced her class. My English lit professor on the other hand was just a nerdier replay of my English teachers from high school. He said he was an expert in Shakespeare and all of our ideas were not valid especially if we were actors. He was then and still is on my "I don't like you list".

I took Spanish for 2 semesters as was required for my degree. I learned more Spanish in the first semester than I did in 3 years in public school. Ninety percent of my classes were awesome. Aside from English lit, the only professor that I did not like was my world history professor. He couldn't hear on account of being a sniper in Vietnam. He claimed to speak fluent Latin and I found is pronunciation to be horrid in my opinion. I did not like his interpretation of history either; I thought he was biased and rather incorrect leaning heavily conservative, Western and Christian. It is because of this professor that I decided not to major in history, and to instead only major in business.

I chose my major because I thought that a business degree was the best chance I had to become something more that what I had been born to do. I also chose that major because I was tantalized by the lure of riches from investing in stocks and bonds. So I declared my major as being business with a financial emphasis. I was planning on becoming either a stock broker or a movie producer. That is until I read a book by Michael Lewis that he wrote about his time in a bond brokerage in New York during the junk bond fiasco in the late 1980's. That book changed my life. It actually set me on my current path, although at the time I did not see that coming.

I actually remember one day when I went to see my advisor. I was planning on going into financial services to learn how to be a stock broker, and I wanted to know what classes I would need to take. He looked at me, and saw that my hair was falling out and I seemed exhausted. In a very polite way he told me that I would be stupid for going for the upgrade and that I should just stick out my current major since I was almost done. I followed his advice.

As to why my hair was falling out, that is a story in itself.

Remember that I said I had studied Aikido starting in the seventh grade? My sensei had left Utah due to a work transfer when I was in ninth grade. His senior students took some of the students that were nearest to them and started their own dojos. So I went with the one that I had the greatest connection with and I continued my study of Aikido. Very soon I started taking Jujitsu from the same man along with Aikido. By the time I was 16 or 17, the Aikido had been phased out and I was exclusively learning Jujitsu under the orders of my new sensei.

Things seemed to be going great with the class. I was learning and remembering and my skill was increasing quickly. When I went to college the senior student of the class seemed to get really mad at me. It might have actually been warranted; I was kind of a jerk. One day we were doing a technique called "hair grabs" in which the attacker grabs the hair of the victim. To execute the technique the victim "breaks" the knuckles of the attacker and drags them to the ground. In class we were supposed to let go, this senior student did not let go. When she finally did let go of my hair, she pulled her hand off of my head and took about a hundred strands with her damaging my scalp. I very slowly started going bald. This happened at the age of 21 or 22. I started using hair re-growth drugs and home remedies, but they only stemmed the tide at best. I chose to start shaving my head the spring before my move to California.

As I wrote before, at Westminster there was always something going on. One of the assemblies I attended was for a mentalist. The man touted that he could read our minds just by picking up on subtle cues from our postures and speech patterns. Being a psychic, I figured I could give him a run for his money, so when he called for volunteers my hand shot up. He called me down to the stage and had me introduce myself. I decided to change my accent and my mannerisms to add a layer of difficulty; if he noticed he did not seem to mind. The first thing he had me do was to think of a 6 letter word and write it down on a hand-held white board for the audience to see. I figured that he would assume that I would pick a word that everyone picks like "banker", "beamer" or "mostly". I decided to be mean and pick a word that does not exist in English, if it exists at all—mostil. This is actually a name, I found this out after the fact; however, I did not know it at the time. He actually got it. The weird thing is I could actually feel him poking around in my head looking for the answer, so let him have it. He asked me if it was a real word. "Not in English." The crowd erupted in laughter.

The next thing he had me do was to cover a steel spike that was set in a large wooden coaster with a Styrofoam coffee cup and then to do the same with 2 similar coasters that were missing a spike. Then he had me mix them up. I actually confused myself and lost track of the spike. When I told him that I was finished, he began to scan me and the mess I had made. He told me that he was getting a lot of conflicting information from me as he raised his hands above 2 of the coasters. I said, "Be careful," and the crowd erupted again in laughter. He then sighed and slammed his hands down on the outer 2 coasters. I completely expected to see blood. He was fine. He removed the center cup revealing the spike, and the crowd clapped loudly.

In my last year at Westminster I decided to take a class that changed my life. At Westminster there is a special term called “May Term”. This is a month long set of classes that are meant purely for enrichment. The cap is 6 hours and the classes themselves are easy. The only way you can fail them is to be exceptionally stupid. This term is responsible for me picking my financial emphasis and learning how to play markets. Then in my last year I had 2 hours left and I didn’t want to take any other business classes; then I saw a class offered by the nursing department about complementary and alternative medicine. I figured why not, it was something that I had always been interested in and I already knew reiki so I took the class.

I was home—I even said that in class. During one of the classes we had a guess speaker that was a massage therapist; not a masseuse that is code for prostitute. Please show some respect and call the people that do legal licensed massage a massage therapist. She had the class do some basic massage on each other. When she came to me and saw my work she said that I had talent and should look into doing this as a career. So I decided to pursue the idea. After I graduated in winter of 2005, I started massage school in January of 2006.

Before I left Westminster I did one last thing of merit. I participated in a study about the effects of meditation and the retention of information. The guy leading the meditations was the total hippie type, but a really great guy. The study was organized by a graduate student in psychology at Westminster and included a sampling of the student population that seemed to be an accurate cross section. I learned so much about myself in that study that I can honestly say for the first time in my life I was actually happy.

When I graduated from college, my parents threw me a party in celebration of my achievement. I was after all the first male in my family to not only attend, but graduate from a 4 year institution. My cat, Richie, hosted the event for me. He walked up to every single person and greeted them. Had he been a human this hello would have been something like this: "Hey, welcome. I'm Richie your host. If you need anything please let me know. Beer and food is in back. Y'all have a good time now." That tuxedo wearing cat (his fir was in the pattern of a tuxedo) made that party. He has since passed away, and during the time of the writing of this book. I miss him greatly, God rest him.

I've already spoken a little bit about massage school concerning C. B. and his meditations. During school I started going to his practice for a meditation group and I learned how to remove bad things from my mind. I was at this time meditating at least 30 minutes a day and I thought I was good and clean until I moved to California.

Elsewhere in massage school, I excelled. I loved the work. In my very first massage there or anywhere, I was on the table. During the massage one of my classmates bent my knee while I was face down. She turned away to get some lotion; when she turned around my knee was still bent and my foot was in the air. She told me to just relax. I replied, "I am relaxed." I did eventually learn how to not just relax but rest. It took a lot of time, meditation and therapy and some people might argue that I'm still doing it, but I'm now a completely different man.

In massage school I learned many things. I learned how to read a person's body with my hands, and not in a sexual way. I learned how to treat a person just by touching them. I learned not just Swedish massage, but I also learned Qi Gong, Cranio-sacral, Shiatsu, Polarity which is not my favorite, Accutherapy which has nothing to do with the Chinese meridians, and a weird meditation technique. I also memorized almost the entire human body, which is still something I hold pride in knowing. When I graduated from school, I decided to take on the world. I also decided to save up some money so I could become a doctor, but that is a story for later.

THE COALMINES OF SANDY

I got my first job when I was 14 working as a janitor at my middle school. I was given a route of classrooms, and my task in these rooms was to sweep and empty the trash. That's all. I did the job very well at least as far as I thought. I was only paid for an hour and a half of work at the rate of $5.15 per hour. Terrible wages right? For a kid, I was a Rockefeller. I was proud of my work and happy that I was making my own money. The downside of the job was if I went over my time I would not be paid for extra time, so it gave me an incentive to be fast. I did not always succeed.

I actually did have a good time with the crew, and I even got to work during the summer cleaning the entire school and making a good amount of money. One of the best days of that time was the chance that I got to use a power washer. Oh my god was that thing fun! We used it to clean the locker rooms and attached bathrooms. It was like having an ultra-powerful water gun with unlimited ammo. I wanted to take it home with me.

I eventually became one of the main people on the crew and I got one of the higher level routes that included the major bathrooms and the teachers' areas. Ladies I am sorry to say that the girls' room is worse than the boys'. I regularly had to wash menstrual blood off the walls and mirrors during my route. At worst the boys just didn't flush the toilet; the girls did that and worse. It was actually thanks to this job that I have the strong stomach that I do. I carried this job off and on for nearly 4 years.

I got my second job at sixteen. I was tired of cleaning toilets, and I wanted to do something with steadier hours. So I went to work for a pizza chain by my house. I was apparently the only person there that knew what hygiene was, and I was the only person not addicted to something. I worked as a cook in back making pizzas. I stunk after work. My cats loved me though. I was making $5.50 an hour and working my ass off. I was working 20 hours a week, and starting to sacrifice my study time. One night I was ordered to close. It was a school night and I got out of work at about midnight. I had a test the next day and I failed it. I quit the immediate day after.

I immediately started working at the local grocery store as a bagger. My wage dropped to $5.15, but the hours were better. The problem with the job was it was surprisingly back-breaking. I was not allowed to wear a coat outside when I was gathering carts during a snow storm. I was not allowed to wear shorts during the severe summer heat that hits Utah in the middle of July. My shoulders were torn up from loading carts, and I was honestly the only one that did any real work. There was this one girl that I "worked" with, every single shift that I worked with her she would spend the entire time trying to figure out her schedule for the next week or month.

Many people think I'm lazy, because they always see me resting. The truth is I work a lot and I distain laziness. She was lazy. When you have job you work; you don't try to get out of work. If you don't want to work or don't like what you do, then just quit and give the position to someone else. In fact I get really upset when people whine about having a job. I know what it is like to be unemployed for an extended period of time, and I value my work. So if you want feel free to join the bread lines, and I will do your job. Sound like a deal?

I eventually got sick of people assuming I was stupid because of my job—baggers are not known for their intelligence—and having torn up shoulders. So I quit and started my first gig in telemarketing. I lasted about a week and quit. Then I found a job that was evidentially perfect for me. I started working as a busser at a local restaurant. This was a famous place known for ribs and peppers. I walked in and got the job pretty much that day. I was back in food service, but now I only cared about the dirty stuff.

I actually enjoyed my job, believe it or not. The crew was great. The job was easy, all be it exhausting. I did make good money though. Fifty dollars for a night shift was nothing and thirty on a day shift was about average. I worked 2 to 3 shifts during the school year and about 5 during the summer. I felt so rich. I was really dirty though. For some reason no matter how hard I tried I could not keep myself clean. I always left work with my clothes hit with at least a little bit of salsa or cheese or something. My cats really liked me again especially after I handled a lot of fish. I bought a pair of shoes that I had to wear for work so I wouldn't slip. I almost never cleaned them and I managed to wear them until the day that I quit. In fact on my last day of work after 4 years there, the last thing that I did was to throw the shoes in the dumpster before I left. As I did this I said, "I will bus no more, forever."

My crew was cool. We would constantly joke around with each other and do stupid stuff the make the night go faster. Dirty jokes were common. One of my favorites was you hold your finger up to a person's nose and say, "What does this smell like to you?" I had several of the servers fall for the finger on the chest gag. Always a good one. Even the managers were halfway decent. My favorite was "Senor Gallo" which is Spanish for "Mister Rooster". We also called him "Captain Underwear" due to his last name. He was one of my better managers and a really great guy.

I eventually worked my way up to being the head of the bus crew and just under the manager of the crew. I was basically a lieutenant if that makes sense. I was in charge of training new bussers and evaluating their work. Believe me, I worked with some idiots. We had this one kid come in and finish training without a problem. His first solo shift he showed up drunk. He sat down in a booth and puked on the table after he hiccupped. Then he got up went into the bathroom and puked again. Then to top it off, he called the manager from inside the bathroom and said he couldn't come in because he was sick. Suffice it to say, he was fired. I picked up the rest of his shifts and laughed about how dumb he was.

We had another kid start working a few days before the Fourth of July. I could tell he had a big chip on his shoulder, but I thought nothing really of it. So the holiday rolled around, and I worked the morning shift. The restaurant was packed and I busted my ass. By the time the night shift rolled around, I was exhausted. The new guy came in and wanted to have the night off so he could go to a barbeque. We told him that we needed him to work, because we would be packed again. He stayed on for about 3 hours. After a nice long break I came back on and found his headset at one of the bus stations. He had deserted. We wore headsets to communicate with the front and the managers; it made work much more efficient and it was my idea although I got no credit for it.

After four years of cleaning tables I started to get a little tired of it as you can imagine. I was still a year away from being legally able to serve due to Utah's weird alcohol laws. In Utah if an establishment serves alcohol of any kind no one that carries the drink to the table can be under the age of 21. Yeah I know...it's stupid. So I quit. My managers said I was stupid for doing it and that I would be back. They were half right.

The following week I started at a call center in downtown Salt Lake. I was told in the interview that I was not doing telemarketing, and that for every call that I closed I would receive an incentive of cash money. They lied. It was in fact telemarketing, and I was not only not getting an incentive other than they would allow me to keep my job, but I was being paid in peanuts practically.

The job was calling on behalf of a mortgage company and trying to get people to refinance their homes at a lower rate. My orders were to call up people on this list that they had allegedly been part of and prequalify them for this lower mortgage rate. If I did well, then I could get a promotion and become a loan officer on the other side of the call center. I started at about $10 per hour and after a year and a half worked my way up to a little over $15. This was a racket. I had to stretch the truth to get people to give me the information

I needed to send them over to the loan officers. People would yell at me, swear at me and demean me; you know what you do to a telemarketer. I'm pretty sure that I even called a few people while they were having sex.

Really people you answer the phone while you're doing it? That's gross and rude.

Seriously.

There was another account that I loved working. It was debt management and assistance. These people were in theory expecting our call, and several were. Every now and again I would get a kid that was playing on the net and filled out the questionnaire as a joke. No real big deal actually. I performed very well with this account, and had a lot of fun with it. I was so good that my boss gave me exclusive rights to call on the debt account. Then after about a month I got a little team that I trained and in effect commanded.

Huge ego boost.

Things started to get a little weird there during my senior year of college. The calls that we were making started to make less sense, and I got the feeling that something wasn't quite right. My hours got slashed randomly. I would show up for work, and then they would send us all home an hour into the shift. Most of the people I worked with when I started were about my age with the youngest being like a year under me and the oldest being middle aged. During this time most of the crew was still in high school. It was actually getting to the point where it was costing my more money to go to work than I was getting from work. So I quit. And a good thing too, the center closed due to the company owner getting nailed for fraud and embezzlement. I hope to this day that I did not contribute to that; not for any legal thing, it's mostly a karmic thing.

Almost immediately that summer I started working as a server (or waiter in the old and real dialect of English that most people speak) at an Italian chain restaurant. It's known for a big bowl of pasta and a place where suburban white people go for a real "Italian treat". Please, that place is about as Italian as my American/Japanese car. We had to attend a training class where we had to memorize the entire menu with ingredients. Italian food is very simple; this was some of the most complex food that I have ever seen. My family sauce only has 8 things in it unless I want to show off. So as I said—not real Italian food.

Also we had to push wine as part of our table greeting. This poses a problem in Utah, mostly due to the fact that most of the people that live there are Mormon and Mormons do not drink. They do not understand alcohol of any kind, because it is not part of their culture. There is not anything wrong with that, but I did feel stupid when I walked up to a table and offered them wine, and watched as their eyes got big and looked at me like I was asking them to sacrifice a puppy to Satan. I eventually just stopped bringing wine to the table; my boss was not happy.

After about 2 months of work there I came to hate my job. I made mistakes that nobody told me were mistakes. I would get yelled at for things that I did not know I was doing. I only had one maybe 2 friends and the rest of the crew hated me. The lowest point of my time there came in the middle of winter when I was on my way for a Sunday lunch shift.

The roads were frozen, but the sun was out. As I set out I got a migraine about halfway to work. I set my car to crawl and I arrived about 45 minutes late. My manager was livid. She walked up to me and asked why the hell I was so late. "Because I have a damn migraine! It hit about half way here. I thought it would be a good idea to drive slowly and actually get here late than drive fast and not get here at all." She backed down and apologized and gave me some painkiller that didn't actually help me because painkillers don't work on me.

I gave my two weeks the week before Christmas and I left. I have not been back since. In fact I don't even remember my last few days there at all, even when I had just left. I even had to keep reminding myself that I quit.

During college I also tried to flex my muscles as an actor. I found an agency in Salt Lake, got headshots and started to go on some really terrible auditions. The scripts that were fed to me were just crap, but I knew that everybody has to do some bad stuff to get their chops to do the good stuff. The agency that I was with was just horrible. Every other month it seemed I got a new agent and I had to audition for them again. The agent would tell me a bunch of stuff that I wanted to hear like I was great and a star and then she/he would ask me to take some acting classes. The first time I figured sure why not, after all even the great ones of Hollywood need formal training to stay sharp and learn new stuff. The class that I took cost me $1400. I didn't learn a damn thing. I eventually lost my patience with them and quit acting all together, but not before I did some rather interesting rolls as an extra.

The first gig that I had was for the season premiere of a show that I had never seen but heard of. The star of the show was in New York and I was part of the background. The production company came into Salt Lake and turned the area into the Lower East Side. It was amazing.

The second gig that I got was for a movie about ice skating and falling in love or something. I played a high school kid in a prep school. I was 21 at the time and only cast member that could actually drink there. My friend Sara and her boyfriend also worked with me on the shoot. The location was amazingly at Westminster. The movie often plays on a cable syndication channel.

I was then sent on the worst audition of my entire time in the industry the following spring. Some guy named "Spanky"—by the way that name was a warning sign—wrote a pretty decent script. It was a teen/college comedy. He was also the director and lead camera. I auditioned for him, but didn't get the part, so I was made into an extra. I was told to report to a grunge/rock/Goth/metal club in Salt Lake for a shoot. I was told to wear something that would be good for a concert. I arrived early because I assumed that I would have to get into makeup. I was the first one there. The rest of the extras arrived about 20 minutes after I did. We waited for a full hour for our director to arrive. When he finally did arrive, he said that he took the wrong exit and got lost. Yeah right. He then sent us into the club for the shoot. The club that we had been sent to was a teenage emo club. The band was terrible heavy metal/Goth fusion music. The place was filled with kids that were "rebelling" as in they were dressed in a rather conformist suburban Gothic kind of way. I watched “Spanky” get his shots and try to record the dialog between his stars. The music was way too loud and it was impossible to hear anything. When we wrapped for the night I was ecstatic.

The last one that I did was for a movie about a woman who grew up Amish but went away to the big city. She came back for a funeral, and got in touch with her past. I actually had a great time with this one. The woman that starred in the show was knockout, and I told her that. The crewmen were surprisingly very respectful of all us extras. I was picked to be a waiter in a restaurant, and just move around in the background. As a joke my name tag was set as “Courtney”. One of my friends, Nic, was there with me. She thought it was hilarious and has called me by that joke name ever since. She is the only person permitted to call me that, so don’t try.

The next job that I got was a result of my management class in college. My professor knew a guy that back in the early nineties created a philosophy in economics that he claimed was based on alchemy. Being that I had studied the basics of alchemy I was intrigued, and then slightly disappointed with what it actually was. The whole idea behind is system was just the efficient use of resources. Still the way he explained the system impressed me, and he told us about a new venture that he was taking on in Salt Lake. I jumped at the chance. It involved life and health insurance that allowed people to buy their own benefits. I thought it was revolutionary, because I had grown up knowing only a company could give people medical insurance. I begged him for information and for the chance to join his company. He gave me a website and a phone number. I got an interview and got the job. I was set to start a few days after the New Year 2006.

I walked in for my first day of work expecting to be trained on what I was doing. I was instead given a notebook with a series of brochures laid out inside. I asked him what this was, and he told me it was my training manual. That day was the first day for our company to go live with a major retail store chain that at the time was known for a big happy face and super low prices. This store chain had started offering health insurance to its employees and special members. My job was to prequalify these people and weed out who was not suitable for us to sell insurance to. I took a new call once every 30 seconds for 8 hours straight with no break. This was actually not a problem; for me I was used to heavy hours and lots of adrenaline while I was making money.

My boss loved me and the crew. We performed admirably. Over the next few days I started learning how to become an agent. My boss gave me materials like a book and some software for me to study. I was told that I had a month to learn all that I needed to know to pass the state licensing exam and become one of his agents. Now here's the thing about the company that I was working for: I thought when I started that there were several hundred people in the office to handle not only the flow from the retail chain but also their regular selling, there were barely a dozen.

Had I known this information I would have quit after the first day. My boss pulled in long term temps and started pressuring me to study harder. He needed agents fast. The retail chain started calling in randomly to assess how we were doing. On one occasion the rep actually yelled at me for answering the phone after allowing two rings. My boss then yelled at me for not doing my job, even though I he had given me conflicting orders and told me to do that and only that.

I was given a script to follow, however it was not built or tested for the real world. I was told to prequalify people, but not to deny them or to allow them to pass. I had no choice but to figure out my own way of doing my job. I should also probably mention that I was attending massage school at the same time. At best I got 6 hours of sleep per night. My schedule was up at 5 AM to work by 7 AM. Leave work at 5:30 or 6 and then arrive at school down the street. I got out of class at 10:30 and arrived home at eleven. I would eat and go to bed, to get up the next day and do it all again. I don't care who you think you are, no person can sustain that schedule for long and not have something happen to them.

After a month and a half I went from being a happy-go-lucky guy to being huge jerk. I was snapping at my mom and dad. I refused to play with my cats or my friends. I was just surly in general. Something had to give. The last week of January my mom broke her knee because I was too tired to help her with clearing the snow. I called in sick for a few days so I could care for her. Guess how my boss felt. My dad being the sweetheart that he is, bought my mom some tiger lilies so she would feel better.

We had recently gotten a new kitten because my cat had died the previous October from renal failure.

This kitten who we named “Oscar”, loved to get into plants. While he was teething, he would chew on the house plants, and the tiger lilies were no exception. There is something very important about tiger lilies that I need to mention in case you don’t know, all lilies including tiger lilies are poisonous upon ingestion and the toxin causes renal failure.

I first suspected something was wrong with Oscar when he crawled into my lap and lied down. He was a rambunctious fuzzy kitten that hated to be held, and now he was voluntarily sitting in my lap. I picked him up and he was listless. My dad and I ran him to the animal hospital and got him admitted. They said he was very ill. No kidding. He didn’t even resist when they put the IV in his neck. The doctor asked us if he had eaten anything out of the ordinary. We didn’t know so I called home and asked mom if there were any flowers littered on the table. There were. My heart sank. I told the doctor to do whatever was necessary to save his life and money was no object. I was making $25K; I was as rich as ever. We left Oscar there to be saved and we went home. I was distraught. It had only been a few months since Daniel had died and now I was going to lose another cat. I couldn’t take it. I did some long distance reiki on Oscar and I prayed.

During my prayer I passed out from exhaustion and I had what most people would call a dream. In this dream I was standing in a big temple lit by torches on the walls. In the center of the main hall was a big caldron and standing over it was the statue of the most beautiful woman I had ever seen dressed in full battle regalia. The statue moved and began to shrink. As it got smaller it came to life and greeted me. She said to me, "Hello my son, how may I help you?"

I knew who this was it was Azna, the Mother of all creation. I said to Her, "Mother, it's my kitten Oscar, he's dying. Please spare him."

She smiled and said to me, "You want me to save the life of an innocent. You must pay a price for this. You must choose between your money and the life of a kitten."

I didn't even think, "I choose Oscar."

She smiled and replied, "Very well, I shall spare his life, but remember the bargain you have struck with me today."

The next day I got a call from the animal hospital. Oscar was out of the woods, but he was acting really scared and he was cowering in his cage. So I drove down. When I got to his cage, Oscar saw me and almost jumped into my arms. He kissed me and nuzzled me and brushed me with his tail. I got an examination room for us, so I could hold him and do some reiki. Oscar was so happy. He sat on my lap and jumped off many times. I was elated so see that he had survived. After about an hour the doctor came in and asked if she could take out Oscar's IV and then we could go home. I said sure, and she took my kitten into the backroom. I heard what was the feline equivalent to "YOU BITCH!" as the IV was removed. Oscar would be just fine. I paid the bill and packed Oscar into my car and took him home. I fought back tears the whole way, and I fell completely in love with that little kitten.

The next day at work, my boss called me into his office. I was expecting him to yell at me, like he had been doing just about every day for the last month or so. I walked in there with my shoulders high and expecting to get chewed out; instead he said that he was letting me go. I was very confused, but my shoulders suddenly dropped about 4 inches. He ran down the list of everything that I had done including the fact that I had not sat for the test yet. I do maintain that this was not my fault other than I just wasn't into it and couldn't pass the practice tests. I smiled and said that he was right and I shook his hand. I walked out of the door with a spring in my step.

Getting fired was one of the best things that ever happened to me. Let me explain. I hated my job and I hated what I was doing. I had to lie to people to get them to buy what I was selling. I was over worked, but well paid in my opinion. When I got home that day I had a big smile on my face. My mom asked what had happened and why I was home so early. I told her the truth. She didn't quite know what to think of it.

From that day until now however, I have had a lot of trouble making money. My firing came right in at the beginning of the Great Recession that has held the world until so recently. I have not had a truly steady job since my last day at that insurance brokerage. I have had work but it wasn't steady.

During this time I was kind of desperate for money. My dad suggested I go work for the government; when I was in high school that was code for military. Let me rewind. Growing up I was raised to be military. In a lot of ways I didn't have parents as much as I had superior officers. The religion I was part of called itself an army as I have stated before. When I was in high school I took a test called the ASVAB, which stands for Armed Services Vocational Aptitude Battery. I did very well. The navy actually called me and invited me to sit down with one of their recruiters, and talk about my future. I said sure. They were very impressed with my performance, and they said that if I went to the academy I would graduate and start out as officer on ship somewhere. I thought that it was a good idea so I took the physical and failed it miserably. I have horrible knees and ankles and I have asthma that activates when my heart beats really fast. When I was rejected by the military, it was a very sad day in my house indeed.

Now back to the conversation with my dad. We knew that the military was out of the question, and I had a degree so he said I should look around. As I was looking around I found out that the CIA was having a recruiting event at Westminster so I decided to go. The guy sent by Langley sounded like Elmer Fudd. I wanted him to say, "Wascally Wabbit," but it didn't happen. I was intrigued with the idea of working as a spy or even an analyst. After all, I had experience in acting and I learn languages very quickly. So I went onto the website, downloaded the application and filled it out. I put it in an envelope and went to the post office to send it. I stood there at the drop box with the flap open and the envelope in my hand. I heard a little voice in my head that said, "Remember your oath." I must have stood there for 5 full minutes trying to decide if I wanted to move to Langley, Virginia or stay in Salt Lake City. I decided to stay. When I got home I destroyed my application.

I'm sorry to say, but do not take career advice from someone who doesn't know what they want, like my dad.

I concentrated on my schooling until summertime rolled around and my mom started to nag at me to find a job. The only thing I was able to find with my degree was…selling insurance. But there was a catch to this time; I was selling life insurance for the purpose of tax free investing. Apparently if you attach any account to a life insurance policy the storage, use and interest of that account is tax free. At least that's what my recruiter told me. So I bought into his little scheme and got myself a policy worth half a million, and I started attaching investments to it. I also started selling insurance after I got my license.

There was something strange about the way the guy did business. His office was in a perpetual state of "setup" like he was just barely moving in. He really focused on my building a team of agents so I could get residual income from their hard work. He actually seemed not interested in my work to actually sell life insurance, and everybody that I talked to he practically jumped on them and begged them to join our little family of agents. So $1200 later I checked on my policy and it was worth $500. I called in to ask what had happened to all my money, and the rep said there were some administrative costs and the market sucked. I asked, "What about there being a bull-market somewhere?" That didn't always hold true she said. I dropped the policy and lost the remainder of my $1200 and quit the company. I have not, nor will I ever think of selling insurance again. Not to mention I didn't make a dime off of the 3 months I spent with them.

Outside of the meager tips that I made for working on people in the school's clinic, I did not have a means of income until I graduated and started my own business the following year. The business I started was called Heaven's Light Massage. I was using an idea that I had come up with during school that if I aligned myself with Heaven then I would be rich. I was wrong. Getting clients was nearly impossible. I started working out of a head shop in Sandy trying to get people into my office for better work. That eventually failed. I then decided to set up at Westminster College as the sports therapist and I got pushed out by a female adjunct professor who stole all my clients.

I also started working at a massage place known for cheep massages. They charged $40 for an hour's work and I saw $15 of it. Honestly I was just happy to have steady work. It did not last. I met the owner about a month into my time there. He fired me after about 10 minutes from the time he shook my hand. He just didn't like me. I hated the place anyway. I worked my ass off and my tips were usually more than my wages; that's a bad sign. The place actually had a huge turnover; if you were there for more than 2 months you were considered old. Suffice it to say the place sucked.

The week that I got fired, I met a couple from Ukraine that owned a massage place on the far east side of Salt Lake City. The business was named for a branch of Buddhism known for its strange sayings and esoteric nature. They loved me, and I knew that they would treat me well. So I signed on with them and started work. The pay wasn't as steady as the other place, but it was much more and I had something like autonomy. I was actually a contractor that worked for the company instead of being an employee. This was done for legal reasons due to the size of the business. By the way, never work as a contractor unless that is the only way to do your job.

The company was good as far as I could tell. The local economy was still growing even though the US economy was falling apart. So we decided to open up a second location. It was to be 3 times the size of our current place of 2 rooms. I helped them build it. I even used my training in Feng Shui to decorate the space for the purpose of creating absolute calm. I still have pictures of this work, and I am very proud of it. We opened with me as a manager, and no one came in. I helped the Ukrainians staff the place and all the people that I hired left because they weren't making any money. I was loyal because I had nowhere else to go.

I stayed there despite the lack of money until I moved to Los Angeles. In fact I'm still friends with my former employers, and we speak every so often.

GIRLFRIENDS, SISTERS AND ASSASSINS

I have a confession to make: I am addicted to beautiful, strong and intelligent women. The Amazon archetype is just awesome to me as is the Warrior-Scholar type. If you want to know what my type is think Wonder Woman or Athena. It is not necessarily the height but the personality that I enjoy. It wasn't always this way however, and it has taken me a lot of years to get to this point.

I got my first girlfriend when I was just a little kid. Her name was B. She was a year older than me and platinum blonde. She lived in a trailer with her mom who worked with my mom at a local steak house. This girl was so pretty. The day that she moved away with her mom when I was 3, my heart broke.

But not to worry, I had another girl that liked me and we were the same age. Her name was S. Also a blonde, we went to church together and lived in the same neighborhood. She was in love with me. I was always invited to her birthday parties and get-togethers and we hung out a lot together. When we were about eight, she told her mom that she wanted to marry me in the Temple and have my babies. Her mom put a stop to that immediately. As I have said before, there are racists where I grew up, and I was of a lesser race because I wasn't blonde and my dad was Catholic. This woman did not want her daughter to be poisoned by an inferior specimen. We never hung out again. She would become one of my worst enemies during middle school, and she was one of the girls that wanted to see me dead. In fact she was one of the two that got expelled for the written threats that I mentioned earlier.

Besides my mom the major female influence in my life was my big sister. She is 10 years older than me from my mom's previous marriage, so she is my half sister. I tormented her. We would go on road trips and I would sit beside her and stare at her. Even as a baby/child my gaze was so penetrating that it unnerved my sister. I was actually reading her although at the time I didn't know it.

One major event between my sister and me occurred when she met a boy and was talking to him while she was watching me when I was about three or four. As she was flirting with this boy, I started to feel that need that I needed to pee. I told her, "I need to potty." She told me to hold on. I pressed again. She told me to hold it. I asked again for her to take me inside so I could go pee. She refused. So I pulled my pants down and peed on the sidewalk. My poor sister was mortified. She grabbed me by the armpits and rushed me into the house, with a yellow stream going all the way. When my parents got home that night from work, my sister told them about the disgusting thing that I had done. My dad said that maybe next time she should listen to me when I say I need to go.

Most of the memories that I have of my big sister involve her boyfriend/husband. They met during their freshman year of high school. It was love at first sight. My sister likes bad boys with a good boy streak. He fit the bill. As a teenager my brother-in-law was into heavy metal and smoking and drinking. My mom hated him.

He was Southern and called my mom “ma’am”; she did not like that. Eventually however, she got used to it and even I started to use it with the exact same friction from the fairer sex. At the time he was just my sister’s boyfriend. He took me under his wing as a little bro. I did not understand what he was doing. He was trying to give me a thicker skin, but the effect was to compound the damage my dad was doing to me and I became a very combative wuss.

Their high school years were great. They had a lot of really good friends, and I was kind of a mascot for the group. I always had fun when I was out with my sister and her friends. They introduced me to movies and ideas and ways of talking and thinking that I would never have learned otherwise.

My sister and her boyfriend both graduated from Jordan High together. The following week my sister moved out, and got an apartment with her boyfriend across town. She started at Westminster College the following fall and they began to create their own life. During this time my sister also became a babysitter for my parents when they had to get away. I loved it. My sister was and is awesome and so were the people in her life. They all contributed to my acting older for better or worse.

When I was 12, my to-be brother-in-law showed me my first all nude magazine. Best day ever for a kid. There were things there that I had never seen, and I wanted to see more, a lot more. My eyes must have remained dilated for days afterward. In a way I do cite that event as the point where my addiction first started, but the internet did push things along. My problem was a lack of control partnered with severe depression. If it wasn't porn that I got addicted to it would have been fighting.

This was during my first few years of puberty. I loved girls even then. Some people thought that I was gay and some still do because I'm not a fan of guns and football and drinking crappy Utah beer. I don't get why what you do is a bearing on your sexual orientation. I don't like football, but I don't like figure skating either. I was part of the boy scouts, but I actually wanted to go out and do things outside, they wanted to stay in and play basketball. I'm as much of a man as anybody, and I don't care what you think.

Beginning in fourth grade I started to like girls. There was a problem however; I had no idea what I was doing. There was a pack of girls that really liked me they would chase me around and generally terrify me with the prospect of pre-teen amore. Every year from fourth to sixth grade these girls would pick about 2 weeks at a time and pester me during recess. I figured out what they were doing way too late and then they would leave. Sadly this would come to be a theme in my romantic life.

By the time middle school rolled around I was firmly convinced that I was ugly and that girls only pretended to like me. Thus, the only way I could ever get a girl to like me was by trickery. Don't do that, it doesn't work. There were a couple of girls that did like me but I didn't realize it.

Then something weird happened. During my ninth grade year, one of my female friends walked up to me while I was at work and asked me to a dance. I said sure, and after the dance we became boyfriend and girlfriend. She was even my first kiss. It was during a rehearsal for *WordRumble*. We were on a break from a scene and playing truth or dare. We were dared to kiss in the girls' bathroom. We took the dare we walked in and she grabbed me by the ears and kissed me nice and light and quick. From that day on we were always together. I was stupid and said some dumb stuff that one of my friends told her about. She dumped me the following week. What was said is unimportant, I learned that nothing is sacred or secret and you should never speak about anyone ever.

I did not get another girlfriend for 2 more years. I did date however, with limited success. I begged an ex-girlfriend of my friend Vairin to fix me up with one of her friends. Never do this. The blind date that I went on was horrible. I actually wished that I had been blind. This girl was taller when she lied down and didn't walk as much as she waddled. She had zero concept of hygiene and smelled like it. Scott did try to warn me that this was a bad idea, but I didn't listen. I have not been on a blind date since, and if you really want to fix me up with someone I want a picture first with astrological information, otherwise, no dice.

Then during the summer before my freshman year of high school I met this chick that was infatuated with me. Her name was T. She was not pretty at all. To her I was something of a god, I guess. She would walk 30 blocks to see me in blazing Salt Lake City summer heat. I thought she was a nice girl, just a little weird. Whenever we were together, she would hold my hand and try to sit on my lab. It eventually got really annoying, and I had to figure out ways to be too busy so she would leave me alone. It took about 6 months but it finally worked.

When I got into high school, I started to actually date. In Utah there is this thing that it is immoral to date if you are under the age of sixteen. So I never technically dated my first girlfriend from the previous year. My first date was with a childhood friend named K. L. She and I were very close, and I wanted to go to the homecoming dance with someone. We were both under 16, but since we had grown up together her mom said that it was fine. My brother-in-law helped me out a lot with the date and even chauffeured for me. I thought we had a great time, and I guess we did.

I did not have another good date for another year, but not for a lack of trying. In Utah men and women do not speak unless it is absolutely necessary or one wants to sleep with/marry the other. The idea is if nothing can come of the event then why do it? It's an attempt to reign in premarital and casual sex, which according to the Church, the major cultural force in Utah, are sins.

Most of the girls I talked to either thought I was disgusting, or some other lame reason like I was the wrong something or other. I started to get desperate and that made things worse. If you really need a date, the best thing to do is not only just be yourself, but to be comfortable with yourself. I could not do this in high school.

I did get to go to prom that year, though. She was a girl in my English class, and I know this is terrible but I do not remember her name. That's fine the date sucked anyway. I asked her out in the usual way that people ask each other out in Utah. This is not simply,

"Will you go to the dance with me?" This will result in a "no". I found that out the hard way. This has to be a grand gesture of some sort. You see, in Utah schools kids don't just ask; they make you work for it. For example: you want to ask a girl to prom so you go to the store and buy a huge jar of mayonnaise and hide your note inside the jar. She has to dig through the goo to find out who asked her. Then she has to reply in some weird way with either a yes or a no depending on how inventive/annoying the form of your asking was. There are many of these including the use of pumpkins (I had it explained to me and I don't get it), toilet papering her yard, defacing his car, a mock kidnapping, poems involving candy, freezing the note in ice, the list goes on and gets rather weird. I used the candy poem method because it was easy and she got something out of it.

So we started to gear up for the big dance. I found out her colors and set my tux rental accordingly. I was gonna look sharp. Then she called me and asked if her friends could be in my group. It wasn't actually my group, it was Scott's. So I called him and asked. He was of course cool with the idea. So the day came around and I picked her up and we met everybody at this tiny Italian restaurant by my house. There were probably 18 of us including the 4 extra people that crashed our group. My date ordered the largest and most expensive thing on the menu; she took 3 bites and said she was done. Then she ignored me. I got upset with her and said, "Excuse me. Hi, I'm your date," and I held out my hand. She seemed confused.

After dinner, we then set out for the Capitol Building in Downtown. The dance was held in the rotunda, and the place looked great. Say what you want about us country types, but when we need to we can make a place look good. My date and I met her friends there. The other two guys and I watched as these three girls ran around that government building taking pictures and acting like skanks. The three of us were mortified and a tinge upset. When I got the pictures I slapped them down on her desk and never spoke to her again.

Something changed my junior year when I met a girl on the first day of theatre class. She was brunette, about my height and moderately attractive. She was interested in me. I figured this was the best I could do so I went for it. This was the worst mistake of my life.

This was The Witch as she will be known in this book. She was from a small town in Utah called Roosevelt. At first our relationship started out great. She was attracted to me. She liked being around me, and I welcomed her attention. There was a minor wrinkle as I came to find out. She had a boyfriend who was in prison for holding up a convenience store, and she actually practiced Wicca. The boyfriend thing was an issue for me, but she said that it wasn't that big of a deal, and besides I was treating her great; better than she had ever been treated in fact. The Wicca thing wasn't an issue to me because she claimed to be a "good witch". So we started to date.

Our first kiss happened as we were walking to lunch and we passed by a service hall in the school. She grabbed me by the jacket and pulled me into the hall. I was then pinned against the wall and my mouth was forced open with hers. I had never known a girl like her in my life; she was exciting and fun and displays of affection weren't taboo.

After that day things became a wash of intense make out sessions, dry humping and magic. I thought I had found a kindred soul. Then I noticed something odd: she was the only person in the entire school that I could not easily see an aura on. So I looked harder, it was chocolate brown. I had never seen one of these before. I had heard of them and they were bad. I figured that it was just because of her past, and in time things would change. I was wrong. It was a warning, and not the first one.

On our first date, the entire night my car radio was playing songs about death, betrayal, and poisons. This is a phenomenon I like to call "psychic radio". Basically I was being warned of this girl, but I didn't listen. I should have dropped her off alone the side of the road and went home. Instead, the date ended at her house with me intending to drop her off, but she didn't get out of my car and I couldn't bring myself to get her out of my car. When 3 AM rolled around and my dad found us. I was ordered back home before he killed me. This was another warning.

I don't actually remember a lot of the relationship. She toyed with my mind so much that I was completely lost. She used sex as a weapon. Although we never slept together and I never saw her naked, I was completely and blindly devoted to her. I was basically hypnotized. Like that's hard to do to a horny teenage boy. She was very insidious. She did a push and pull mental tactic on me that left my mind in pieces, and I'm pretty sure she even cast a spell on me. I'm not going to go into specifics, but when I talked to my friends after the relationship they said I was a different person while I was with her.

Before I continue, I do want to say something. Despite what this girl did to me, I harbor no ill will to anyone practicing the spiritual way of Wicca. I have several friends that are Wiccan, and I have even incorporated some pagan beliefs and holidays into my life. I'm Gnostic, I can do that. She was one of the bad ones, and not a true representation of the Wicca religion at large.

Moving on.

During our romance I held an office in FBLA—Future Business Leaders of America. What, I was a nerd. Our club was chosen to host the homecoming dance that year. So of course I jumped in. We threw a great dance complete with balloon drop. The Witch was my date. People that hated me were embarrassed for me, because of how out of myself I was. I thought she was gorgeous in her dress, everyone else said she was in a word—not. Not long after homecoming, FBLA had a conference in Park City, which is a tiny ski town east of Salt Lake. I didn't actually want to go, but I went anyway. During the conference on the last day I met a girl at a dance from another school. She was gorgeous, and interested in me. She voluntarily gave me her number. I never called her. Had I not been so blinded by The Witch, my junior year would have been very different and possibly better.

Strange things did start to happen as her hold on me began to be broken. One of these involved a medallion with an embossment of John Paul II. This medallion was actually with me the day that I got hit by the car, and I have kept it as a good luck charm. It is currently sitting in my pocket as a key chain. During my time with The Witch I lost the medallion, and it turned up in the drawer of my aunt across town. My aunt had actually given it to me after she had bought it in Vatican City. This was a rather big thing for me. After I lost my medallion, I tried to break up with The Witch, but I couldn't do it. I was disarmed.

She moved away to a small town in Utah Valley, and broke my heart. The day she left and broke up with me, I went home and I did something drastic. I literally crawled up the stairs and dropped my bag off somewhere along the way. I went into the kitchen, and I picked up my favorite knife. It was long and never dulled. I held it in both hands and pointed the tip at my heart. The only reason I didn't go through with it was I remembered what I had learned in biology class that week. We had learned that in order to break the thoracic wall a great deal of power must be used, and since muscles only contract, by cutting those muscles I would lose all the strength that I would need to end my own life. At best I would suffer and bleed for a few hours. So with a trembling hand I set the knife down on the counter and slumped into a sobbing heap on the kitchen floor.

I was ordered to seek counseling. I did and I considered the problem resolved. I was wrong. Sporadically, The Witch would come back into my life, and each time she would meet nothing but hate and distain from me. As far as I am concerned she is the cause of my suicide attempt, and it was her will.

The following summer the remnants of The Witch's influence on me affected my family. My dad and

I started to sense that somebody was watching us. We both wrote down what we thought we had seen and felt. With the exception of the words used the description was exact. It was the spirit/ghost of a cowboy smoking a cigarette and standing in our driveway. He was corrupted. We told him to leave and he said no. We attacked him without effect. Then my mom had an idea: destroy everything that The Witch had given me. It worked. The cowboy left and there was peace in our house again.

After The Witch, I had nothing. I wanted no contact with any girls at all. Then I met C. S. at an SAT session at the university. She was hot. She had long curly brown hair and big brown eyes; gorgeous skin and an awesome smile. She was a theatre geek like me, and she came from another school. Everything fit, so I asked her out. We started to date. Amazingly she was Mormon but didn't act like it. She was still a good girl, but she wasn't prissy as far as I could tell.

When I went to pick her up for a date at her house I expected basically what I had grown up with. She was much richer. The house her family lived in was at the mouth of a canyon called Big Cottonwood Canyon that opens to the Salt Lake Valley. I thought I had hit the jackpot. She was hot, smart, fun and rich. I started to fall for her. I took her to a dance at my school that was girls' choice, and inadvertently embarrassed her. Our relationship spiraled out of control, and I was the cause. I was very depressed and she bore the brunt of my suffering. We stopped seeing each other near the end of senior year, and I didn't speak to her again for a full year when I became an Elder in the Church. She developed a crush on me at that time, but I shut her down because of what I had learned about astrology. I will get to that in just a bit.

After C. S., I met a girl from Berlin. She was okay. Her main appeal was the fact that she was very intelligent and spoke several languages and she wasn't Mormon or a virgin. You'd think I would learn. This girl did nothing but talk. She would talk for hours at me on the phone, and I would get to speak every so often. We were dating, but she lived on the other side of town and I was poor so we didn't get together that much.

One night I was talking to one of my friends, and he offered to read my cards over the phone. I said sure. He asked me if I was seeing somebody. I was. He then said she was cheating on me. I knew who it was, she had told me about a guy that had come to her school on an exchange program from Germany. She spoke very highly of him. I called her immediately and confronted her. She said that she was with him, and that if I proved my love for her by agreeing to follow her back to Germany when she graduated the next year that she would marry me. I told her no and lost her number after that. And a good thing too; she had told me that she had been raped before and her uterus was scared as a result of an infection. There is only one disease that I know of that can do that—Chlamydia. Had I actually slept with her I would have caught it and been poisoned for the rest of my life.

Things were really quiet until I got into college.

Her name was Saralee, Sara for short. I met her through college at the freshman campout. She was this little brunette with an awesome body, and wow was she smart. I was instantly smitten. She was however a bit thick headed; I hit on her 5 times before she realized I liked her. On the last day we went on a hike together that was about 14 miles and ended up holding up the entire bus train. During that hike she taught me something. I had learned about the astrological signs before, but I didn't know how they interacted. She told me how. I'm a Libra. Sara is a Taurus. We are different enough that a relationship between us that is not only sexual but friendly as well is very difficult. She said she would gladly be my friend, but never my girlfriend. Her logic was flawless. We have been good friends ever since.

I took what Sara taught me that day, and researched it further. I realized why all my ex-girlfriends and my relationships with them were the way that they were. It wasn't necessarily because I was an idiot. It was because I was incompatible with them in the first place. Three of my exes are Capricorns. We are incompatible because of the fact that Libra is an air sign and Capricorn and Taurus are both earth signs. Air and earth are polar opposites; therefore we can either just have sex or just be friends, not both.

Well, that isn't exactly true. No relationship is certain. Every relationship requires work, and every relationship requires sacrifice. Whether or not you are willing to make the necessary changes and compromises and still like each other let alone love each other is what makes it possible. That goes for "compatible" and "incompatible" signs and people across the board. I use astrology as a means of an educated guess to how a given person will behave, but there is this little annoying thing called "free-will", and it changes everything.

After I had my talk with BGR about fashion, I asked Sara for help in designing me a new wardrobe. I asked her because she was an artist, and I trusted her not to dress me like a fool. So we went out to a few places and she showed me how to match colors and patterns. She also enlisted the assistance of her two best friends, Christine and Tara. They gave me great information and I used it well. There was an unintended side effect however. I developed a crush on Tara. I am not proud of this.

Tara was very beautiful. She had long blonde hair and big brown eyes. She was tough, smart and a bit of a geek. She liked me as a friend at best. I tried to date her but kind of turned into a stalker. When she got married about a year or so later to a great guy, we sat down and she said that what I did was not my fault *per se*. It was something that had happened to her a lot with guys, and that it was just as much her problem as it was mine. We made peace and are friends now.

Now as I said before, the girls at Westminster College are awesome. They are some of the most beautiful women that I have ever seen or met. I had a new crush almost every single day. During lunch and dinner time when the dormmies would come down to find food, I felt like a bear in a salmon run. There were so many that I couldn’t pick. As a result I didn’t date a lot in college due to my hesitation and low self-esteem.

For the guys: unless you at least try you will never know; always go for the hottest most unattainable woman you can. Who knows, if you hit it off she might be the love of your life. That being said, make sure you can actually stand to be around her. I have actually been out with a model. We went on two dates. I realized she was an idiot, so I dumped her. I met this girl not long after I learned how to do something that I will talk about in just a little bit.

I finally came across this philosophy of throwing caution to the wind when I was in my junior year of college. I asked a girl out that Sara had set me up with. She was a tiny brunette named K. F. Man was she cool. We started off great. She liked ghosts and psychic stuff, and she was into having fun. The problem was she had a disease in her lungs called cystic fibrosis. On our second date, she said that she was living on borrowed time and she did not know when she was going to die. She didn't want me to go through that pain so we broke up. I have no idea where she is now, but I suspect she is dead.

Right after K. F., I met another girl named K. B. This girl was even better. She was blonde and smart as hell, all be it a little scatterbrained. She worked out. She could hold a conversation. I thought she was awesome. We connected astrologically and spiritually. She was actually pagan, and it was because of her that I started to observe holidays like Samhain and May Day, and I still do. I wanted to date her, but she wasn't interested. I was kind of a jerk, and she didn't want to get her heart broke by me. She also didn't want to hurt me. We are now friends. She is currently in Africa as part of the Peace Corps, and having a great time from her mass emails to home.

During my senior year I met a girl in the mediation class that I took as part of a study. H. D. was different. She was a short and densely built blonde. She was okay as far as looks and personality were concerned.

When we first met she was very nervous around me, in fact the first sentence she said to me took her almost half a minute to say. That would not last however. When she got comfortable with me, she developed a rather sharp tongue, and she would make fun of me on a daily basis. One day she called me a wuss or something, and I retorted, "At least I don't play a game that is marketed to twelve-year-olds." She was fascinated with an online collector game about weird animals that was designed here in the States. She spent more time playing online games and poker with her girlfriends than she did with me. See, girls can be self absorbed too. I bought her a birthday present, which she rejected. She got me nothing. So I dumped her after my friends begged me to do so.

Guys and ladies: no one will respect or love you if you don't respect or love yourself first. It has taken me a long time to really learn what that means.

After Westminster, I went to massage school and met some actual women, but nothing other than a little brother/big sister relationship sprang up. Then one day Scott gave me a call and invited me to a party he was having in Provo. When I got there I hugged my brothers; this is how we say hello and good bye. Suddenly I was tackled by a tiny brunette with a big smile. She wrapped her arms around me and said, "Hi I'm Cami."

This was Scott's new girlfriend. She was so damn cute; I couldn't help but talk her ear off. We spent the entire party talking. She was brilliant and fun, and I was very happy for Scott to have found her. By the end of the party I had adopted Cami as my little sister, a place she holds to this day.

When Scott had gotten back from his mission, he got into that movie with the swords made out of light. He had bought some of the mock ups of these swords and was talking Cami into sword fights with them. She always lost. So I took it upon myself to teach her how to fight. She had talent. Every time we would spar she would somehow manage to cut me open with a blunt wooden object. I was so proud of her. On one special occasion, I was wearing a jade ring. More on why later. We were sparing out on the front lawn, and her blade came across my finger and cut my ring into two perfect halves. I lost one of the halves and kept the other. As a fighter my little sister is awesome, and I love her deeply. My only regret is that we didn't get to grow up together, and do all the things that big brothers and little sisters get to do to each other.

That does however not mean that I am any less of a big brother to her. When she and Scott broke up, Cami got really depressed. So one freezing winter night, I drove down to BYU, where she and Scott were both going to school, and I took her to my place for some peace and quiet away from her roommates and the memories of Scott. Yeah, by doing that I broke BYU's stupid honor code, but my family was in pain and I came to the rescue. When I walked into her apartment she was sitting on the couch crying while one of her roommates was trying to comfort her. All I said was "Get your coat," and we left. She had her first decent night's sleep in weeks at my place, and we freaked my parents out a little bit. Oops.

Not long after I met and adopted Cami, The Witch wormed her way back into my life. Jon had recently begun dating a girl from the University of Utah; she was hot, I was very proud of him. Her parents were actually quite rich and they owned an actual cabin a few miles south of Park City. So near the end of summer, she invited Jon and all of his friends up for a co-ed sleepover weekend. I was at Jon's front door before he hung up the phone from the invite call.

I volunteered to drive some of our friends to the event. The only one that didn't have a ride already figured out was The Witch. My friends told me don't worry she's changed. They were right—she was now better at what she did. She and I jumped in my car and set out. She threw herself at me the whole time, and I denied her.

At the cabin we didn't speak much, I was too engrossed in the card games that were being played and teaching good Mormon boys how to play poker and blackjack. When people started getting ready for bed, I decided to leave because I genuinely had to work in the morning. I said my goodbyes and thanked my hostess. The Witch asked if she could bum a ride from me back to Salt Lake, I said sure. In the car she continued to throw herself at me. She reached out and grabbed my hand while it sat on the gear shift. Instead of squeezing back, I pulled away and she then sat dejected in her seat. When I dropped her off at Jon's place for her car, she asked me if I wanted to make out and maybe do more. I told her no, and drove off. Last I heard of this woman she is married and living in Costa Rica; good riddance to her.

One of the most important women in my life during the last couple years in Salt Lake City was A. M.

We worked together at that massage place I spoke about earlier. When I first saw her, she had just interviewed for a position at our clinic. She had short red hair, big brown eyes and loads of freckles. I thought she was hot. A couple of days later she came in for her first day and we got to talking; we were instant friends. I found out about her birthday; we were not compatible, so we decided to just be friends. This was one of the best moves I ever made. She gave me insights into the female mind that I had never had before. In return, I became her personal psychic. That was a lot of fun; I felt like I could be me without judgment. At work we were almost inseparable and we even hung out outside of work, which is something was I wasn't used to doing. In Utah, most people just go to work, do their thing and go home. You don't make friends with the people you work with; it's seen as being unnecessary. I have no idea why this is so. A. M. and I are still good friends, and I love hearing stories about her 2 daughters.

A few months before I met A. M., I decided to join something of a secret society. They are known for using codenames in chat rooms. One of their "heroes" had a couple of shows on basic cable where he took a bunch of nerds and taught them how to talk to girls. I bought his book and studied it. The stuff actually worked, but the thing was it only worked on girls that had actually had sex and wanted to have sex. It failed on the Mormon girls, because of cultural differences. My friends however thought I was either completely mad or a genius depending on their frame of reference. I started dressing nicer and wearing jewelry including an agate necklace, a ruby in silver ring, a citrine in silver ring and the jade ring that my little sister cut in half. The last thing that I did to complete my transformation into something resembling a man was to shave my head. The idea was that since everyone around me was trying and failing to keep their hair, I should simply get rid of mine. Now I look great.

After my ring was cut in half, I took it to a custom jewelry shop and I asked the girl working there if she could make me a ring out of silver with the jade as a base. She was so cute, so I did my thing and I asked her out. She was not my type. She was a total nerd and not a smart one sadly. I don't mind a girl that's a bit of a geek, but she must be intelligent. The only thing this girl knew how to do on her computer was to play a very popular online role-playing game about the craft of war. I never called her again.

I have since abandoned that society and their methods in favor of something better. Just being me, and not caring what anybody thinks about it. Remember you need to be you if you want anyone to like you or even love you. A person who is only living a partial life will never be happy, and they will always be alone even if they have someone.

My time with women has been difficult, but what man doesn't have difficulty of some kind. Things did get easier in Los Angeles, and something truly awesome happened as a result.

DIGGING IN THE GOLDEN STATE

My decision to leave Utah actually happened just after I graduated from massage school. I realized that I was not going to make it as a massage therapist in Utah due to politics and the fact that I had a pesky little habit of diagnosing people. That is illegal for a massage therapist to do, and at least will result in the dismissal of the license and possibly jail time. So I decided to become a doctor. I knew that the University of Utah Medical Center would never take me due to several factors, and I really didn't want to study Western Medicine. It wasn't that I didn't believe in it; it had actually saved my life. The reason was I didn't want to become a slave to a drug company or an insurance company.

So I started to research Chinese medical schools. There were none in Utah. I did find one in Portland, Oregon, one in Colorado and several in California among other places. Based on culture, climate, cost and local economy I narrowed down my choices to Oregon and California. From there I inquired with each one of the schools and narrowed everything down to either Portland or Los Angeles. This was a total of five schools. It was a crap shoot. I analyzed everything about the cities and the schools. I checked the hard economic numbers and the local astrological climate compared to my chart. Both cities were even when it all boiled down.

I had to figure out something, so I decided to think outside the box. I found a local psychic and I asked her where I should go. She told me I was going to California by way of Los Angeles. I then asked her what school I was going to, and she said that I would go to a school with a green logo by the beach on the north side of the city. That little bit of information completely cut out Portland, and dropped the schools down to only 2 possibilities with respect to location. The logo synched it; there was only one school that fit the description.

A week later I drove down to LA and I started to look for a place to live, a place to work and I spoke to the school. Everything went great; my only concern was when to move.

So I spoke with the same psychic and she said I should wait until the start of 2009. I was warned that things would not be easy, but it would be worth it. I was told that I would meet somebody and be part of many good things. I was told that work would come, but I needed to keep my focus on my school. If I didn't, the consequences would be…bad. The night that I got home from my visit with the psychic I started to pack for my big move.

Over the next few weeks I slowly put my entire life into boxes. I packed up about 5 boxes worth of books alone. I like my books. I have books on many subjects from sociology to magic to medicine to mystery and intrigue. There were about twice as many book boxes when compared with everything else. I stacked all these boxes up in my bedroom and closet and I waited for the year to change.

My cats thought this was very odd. Oscar would jump up on the boxes while I was sleeping and stare at me in the night; he woke me up several times. Richie would come into my room and watch me trying to figure what I was doing and more importantly why I was doing it.

During my packing time I got together with my friends as much as I could. I knew that I was going to miss them and they were going to miss me, so we all tried to soak up as much time was we could. This eventually culminated in a big party in my honor, which gave me enough of a chance to say good bye to everyone properly. That Christmas was the last chance for my family to help me out in a meaningful way. I got a lot of kitchen stuff and basic living things. I was very grateful.

My maternal grandmother had died of heart failure 2 summers before. I was tapped at that time to help my family get her estate in order, such as it was. I actually used my abilities to speak with her father and her mother about the death and where things were hidden in her house. We got everything taken care of. I gave the eulogy at her funeral, and I honored her memory as best I could. It is because of my grandmother that was even able to move to California. She gave me a lot of what I needed as an inheritance. This included a kitchen table, knives, a microwave and many other things that I still use to this day. God rest her.

I left Salt Lake City, Utah at 4 AM local time on January 21, 2009. My parents were to follow me with a UHAUL trailer. So I said good bye to my cats, they just turned and walked away. As I walked out the door my dad grabbed me and gave me a huge hug. That was the only time in my entire life that I have ever seen him cry. Mom was stronger. She said they would see me later that day.

So I put on my coat, my gloves and my hat and stepped out into the frigid Utah morning air. It was about 5 degrees Fahrenheit, which is cold enough to make strong men say, "It's way too cold, I'm not going out there." I got in my car, pointed it south and drove off. That was the hardest thing that I have ever had to do.

As much as I would rather not admit this, I cried hard through about a hundred miles of dense fog. I was terrified and exhilarated at the same time. I wanted to stay with what I knew and loved and even hated, because it was easy. I was leaving everything behind; I may as well have been moving to a different country. I knew that I had to leave. I knew that if I didn't leave the state, I would never amount to anything, because I would have done just as several of my friends had done—move out then come crying back to mommy and daddy when things got rough. I refused to hang my head in shame any longer, so I made one of the biggest leaps that I have yet to make—I moved to one of the hardest cities in the world.

By midday I arrived in Las Vegas. I called my parents to report in. They were about 40 minutes behind me. I ate, gassed up and set out further. When I got to Primm a few minutes later and I was stopped by a road block. Everyone was being detoured into a shopping mall that was by a casino. I was not happy. So I waited for about an hour. Then I decided to go get a burger and I found out that there was a reconstruction going on with I-15. I asked the 2 guys how long it would take and they said about 3 hours. I was due in LA at my apartment in 5 hours. It seemed I would have to wait. My parents pulled in beside me and we sat and waited.

I had since removed my hat and gloves and was now down to just my coat which was unzipped. I felt rather warm. The southwest crows saw all the people funneling into their parking lot, and they decided to make the best of the human situation. They started stealing food from people who were just not paying attention. I thought it was funny as hell.

I arrived in Los Angeles at about six that night local time. The main office to my apartment was closed, so my parents and I found a motel in Marina Del Rey/Venice. Not a bad place. I did get a funny vibe from the area though.

The next day at first light we got up and headed to my apartment. I got my key and started to move in. It was a hot day, about 70 degrees. I didn't need a coat. I dropped into shorts and a t-shirt and sandals and we got to work moving me in. It took a few hours, but when we were done loading all my crap inside, I gave my parents one last hug and kiss good bye and I was finally alone in my own place. It was weird.

That night as I was watching syndicated sitcoms on my tiny TV and my apartment rumbled a little bit. I thought, "Huh that was a big damn truck." About 2 minutes later a news caster came on and said, "There has been a 4.2 earthquake in the Marina Del Rey area of Los Angeles. Please stay tuned for further developments." Welcome to LA was all I could say.

For about the first month and a half I slept in a sleeping bag on top of an air mattress. I had chosen not to bring my bed, because it was full of water being that it was a water bed, and I didn't want to schlep it all the way to LA. You have no idea how sore my back and hips got. I couldn't stand it anymore. I bought a bed and mattress set online. I also bought a couch; I needed something to sit on. I had forgotten to get one in Utah.

As I was getting used to SoCal I did my best to find work. It was proving to be difficult. Nobody was hiring. That didn't make much sense to me. All the economic data that I had said Los Angeles was doing just fine. Life wasn't easy, but it wasn't impossible to find a job. So I reran the numbers. The local Los Angeles economy tanked at about the same time my key slid into the lock of my apartment for the first time. I was now screwed. I almost called mommy and daddy and asked them to come and get me, but then I thought, "No. I'm here for a reason, and that is not to run away." So I stuck it out, and I was rewarded in a way.

Before the reward happened though I had one little thing to do. I managed to get an interview with a company that did bulk phone sales out of Burbank. At least that's what they said they did. I passed the first interview and was asked back for the second. I was told to wear clothing that I would wear to an office, so I jumped into my suit and headed back to Burbank. I actually felt at home in that part of LA. It looks and feels a lot like Salt Lake City.

It was a little cold and rainy that day, but I thought nothing of it; I was going to an interview and what interviews take place outside. After an initial meet-and-greet with people that would eventually become my coworkers, I was assigned to a kid that was going to show me how things worked and we left the office for a mall parking lot. I asked if we were being redirected to a store front, he said that they didn't have a store front. Then he started to change out of his suit and into some street clothes while standing there in the parking lot. In retrospect I should have left at that moment.

So we headed out in his car to a part of LA called Chatsworth, which is a rather upscale community. It's no Beverly Hills, but still these people were pretty well off. When we stopped in his "territory", rain began to fall. He asked if I had any rain gear with me. Why the hell would I have any rain gear, I was going on an interview!? What I actually said was, "no." He said that I was going to get wet. Then he put on a cover for a phone company now known for their smart phones and internet connections. We then started walking around a neighborhood knocking on doors. His personality changed when we were in front of people, I actually thought he was kind of annoying.

We didn't get anything. In the course of this walking around I was getting soaked. The rain was so heavy that I couldn't see more than 50 feet in front of my eyes. After about 2 hours—I was being very generous—I was finished with this dog and pony show. I demanded to be taken back to my car. I was drenched. My feet hurt. I was being "interviewed" by some kid that was kind of shady himself. I did the exit interview with his boss, and I told him in a very nice way that his business was a joke. Sadly, businesses like that were the only ones that wanted to talk to me.

During this time my little sister Cami got into some trouble with her boyfriend and an authority figure.

Never mind what she did or what the issue was, it was bad enough for me to freak out. She called me one day in tears looking for advice or at least a sympathetic ear. I listened to her plight, and I went into protection mode. I told her how to handle the problem, but the more I thought about her issue the angrier I became. I offered to drive back to Salt Lake and kill the offender if needed. I even told her to sit tight I would be there in 10 to 14 hours; I was on my way out the door with keys in hand. Cami managed to talk me down by pointing out that I didn't have the money to make the trip. The issue was eventually resolved amicably, and she did face some penalties even though it was not her fault, but that's just Utah justice for you.

In the end of February, an old acquaintance from middle school found me on Facebook. Her name was D. E. She was interested to see that I was in Los Angeles. She asked me if I was there to be an actor. I told her no, I was there to go to school to become a doctor. She was pleasantly surprised. So she asked me out for a drink in Canoga Park, and I went.

The D. E. that I remembered from middle school was a half Goth chick with major issues. She was a little different now. She was as tall as me, and had this thick mane of brown hair. She had big green eyes and a huge smile. She had adopted a bit of a hipster look, and she had recently taken up smoking. D. E. introduced me to her friend L. Her friend was a typical Swedish blonde. Wow was she hot. I wanted her immediately, but D. E. had pretty much marked her territory with me. So we hung out that night. After the drinking was done, we decided to go for a drive and talk. I took her all the way to Hollywood then back to Topanga Canyon. I dropped her off at her place at sunrise. It was one of the best first dates I have ever had.

I arrived home and slept away the day. My phone rang and woke me up, it was D. E., and she wanted to hang out again. I said I had some time the next day, and I invited her and L. to my place for swimming and sauna time. D. E. showed up sans L. When I asked where she was, D. E. lied to me and said that L. had to work. So we went down to the sauna with a bottle of wine and started hanging out. I'm not going into details, but we ended up making out in the sauna. We decided to leave and head back up to my apartment, where she became my first.

I was terrible the first time, but who isn't. I did get better as we slept together and dated. We were actually pretty good together, at first. About 2 weeks into the relationship D. E. showed up at my place with little things that she needed if she was going to stay for more than a day at my apartment. One of these was bi-polar medication. I decided to make the best of it, after all on her upside was a happy-go-lucky comic book geek. I was not one, but I thought it was kind of endearing. I wouldn't meet her downside for about another month.

Near the end of March I found a job. Things were looking up, and I had D. E. to thank for the boost to my self-confidence. It was with a whole sale company that allows a regular person to buy directly from a manufacturer. My job was to sell the idea to people. I lasted a week and I was laid off due to sudden budget cuts. My boss felt really bad about it, so he had me use him as a reference. His location went under a few weeks later.

After I lost my job, D. E. found a job working as a pharmacy tech in the Valley. I was proud of her. It was about this time that cracks started to appear in our relationship. She had me go to comic book signings for her, and read comic books with her. She also brought over her gaming console. I refused to play it because I had just kicked a rather heavy gaming addiction about a year before. I basically got bored with it, and I realized just how much time I was wasting with a paddle in my hand when I could be doing things with the people that I loved.

Our last good date was our one-month-anniversary date. It was also a date to celebrate me getting a job, which I lost 2 days later. From then on we tended to embarrass each other sometimes just for the hell of it. D. E. wanted me to start going back to church with her; amazingly she was Mormon. I told her no, and under no circumstances. She demanded to know why, so I wrote down all my beliefs and I gave it to her as a manifesto. When she finished reading what I wrote, she messaged me on Facebook and said that she did not respect my beliefs and therefore couldn't be with me. Thirty seconds later I was dumped via the internet.

A few days later she came by to my place to pick up some stuff she had left there for safe keeping. She also told me that she was seeing somebody new. I had actually met the guy just before D. E. and I broke up at a party. He owned a comic book store. I was genuinely happy for her; she had found someone more her type. D. E. is currently married to another guy and living in Arizona. We still speak occasionally, and we're friends. How many people can say that?

D. E. fulfilled a very important role in my life. It wasn't just about sex; she gave me the chance to see what a good relationship looked like. It's sad that it didn't last, but she gave me things that I still have, use and cherish. I thank her for everything she did for me.

I did get a little depressed when D. E. dumped me, but I had more pressing matters to worry about. I was running out of money. I made some calls to my family in Salt Lake so I could get some money. I got enough to inch by month to month. I cut how much I was eating down to 1800 calories, which is enough to carry on basic functions. As a result however, I lost my abilities. The only things that remained functioning were my heightened senses. I had to stop working out, because I could afford to feed the muscle. I became very guarded, and very opportunistic. Instead of driving I walked everywhere. I looked in every single place I could to find a job, but no one would talk to me.

I'm sure you're wondering, why I didn't get help from the food bank, or a soup kitchen or even the Church. All the soup kitchens that I found were located in very dangerous parts of town. I didn't qualify for the food bank as I read it on the site. As for the Church, in Utah and in my experience, there is no help given without the expectation of work being returned. So if I asked for help I would have to pay back that assistance, even if the required task was beyond my skill.

I saw a ray of light when Scott called me and said that he, Jon and a new friend of theirs named N. were coming down for a visit. I invited them to stay with me, and they accepted. We had a great time. I took them to the beach. I took them to UCLA. I even provided them with a GPS so they could go to a Ghosthead convention.

Scott, Jon, N. and W. R. were now totally involved in the cult of Scott's favorite ghost-themed franchise. They had made jump suits and back packs that lit up and had the wands the guys use to capture ghosts. These things are actually very impressive. They spared no expense and were extremely anal on the details. Like I always say, if you're going to do it, do it right.

I could tell the guys were shocked at my transformation. When I lived in Salt Lake, I was body building and aiming for an end weight of 180. I had moved to LA at 155, I was now at about 125. I was starving to death. As payment for my hospitality, the guys bought me enough food to last me 2 full weeks. At least that's as long as I made it last, the way I was eating was miniscule. Had I been eating the way I should have been that food would have only lasted me a few days.

One day as I was driving home from something, I don't remember what, I was feeling like I should just give up and go home to Utah. It would only be shameful if I let it be shameful. I could regroup and start again at a later time when the economy got better. While I drive I like to surf through my preset radio stations in my car. I came to one of my country stations and a song about change and strength was playing. It was written and performed by a young female country star that I have always had a huge crush on. She is known for her curly blonde hair and real life lyrics. As that song played I realized that I had moved to California to do something, and I always finish what I set out to do. People were counting on me, and I could not let them down. Not to mention I was counting on me to not end up like my father. If I ever get the chance to see that young woman face to face I would love to buy her a cup of coffee and give her a big hug.

I needed help, but more importantly I needed money. Then I remembered what the psychic had said, I needed to focus on school and work would come. So I started the application process and got accepted for the summer 2009 quarter. I took out a $25,000 student loan and started eating again. But before I started school and got my money I had something else happen to me.

I got a job at a gym in Hollywood as a personal trainer. It paid eight bucks unless I billed hours for training muscle heads. My first day of work, I learned something and I realized that I had made a colossal error. The gym I was at was a gay gym. I was one of maybe three straight guys in the entire place. I got hit on so many times that I found out what it must feel like to be a woman.

I didn't get to train many people. I was basically told to walk around the workout floor picking up weights and trying to con people into letting me teach them how to do something that they were already doing for free. That didn't go well. I was not trained at all. I was given a video manual of company policy and that was it. I was ordered to report for training 2 weeks after I started work. The problem was this was also my first day of school and they said that they would work with me. Instead they fired me for allegedly not punching out correctly. I think somebody was out to get me and got me fired.

I was livid. I was angry for a week and a half after that. I will never step foot in any of their gyms for as long as I live.

I started school the day after I got fired. It was great. My first class was Qi Gong and my second was Fundamentals of Chinese Medicine. I excelled at both. By the time the summer quarter ended I was eating reasonably well and I was starting to gain weight. My abilities still had not resumed and I was starting to get worried.

You see my abilities are part of me. For you to understand what it is like not having abilities after having them for a life time, imagine being a crowded mall at Christmas time. You are blindfolded, your ears are plugged, your nose is plugged, and you are wearing mittens. Your job is to find the perfect gift for your best friend without getting mugged, raped or taken advantage of. All that I can do was given to me, and I am supposed to use what I was given. How I use my abilities is however open to interpretation, and I have screwed up many times. I will get to the biggest one a little later.

Back when I was trying to become a trainer, I got wind of a company that would pay you for the exchange of a shell corporation that they would then take the rights to for the price of the $2000. I was a little skeptical. So I got the information and drove to the place to check them out. They were legit. So I started the process of the creation of a company that they would then buy. They did all the hard work for me. They came up with the name and pushed the legal paperwork through. The guy that was my contact treated me like a millionaire; I loved it, I won't lie. We had to set up three PO boxes for the company; he and I did that together up in the Valley. That was a good day, he even bought me lunch. I also got to go to my first professional major league baseball game with him and his wife. That was neat. Then he started getting really right-wing on me verging of psycho and I had to cut him out of my life. I do not like extremists in any form. I did get my money and it paid my bills for a month at the time when I needed it most.

I was still living at my first place when I started school. The apartment itself wasn't bad with the exception of the silverfish. My neighbors got on my nerves. They were heavy pot heads. Regularly when I would go out to get my mail I would pass by their door, and I would suddenly get a craving for nacho cheese flavored corn chips. D. E. also met them one day. She thought they were hilarious.

One night at about 11, I was woken up by the sound of something rustling in the space between our apartments. I was worried that my neighbors were being robbed so I opened my door to catch the guys in the act. The two pot heads were loading a couch that they had found on the side of the road into their apartment. I asked them if they would like some help they said sure. When I asked where they got the couch, they said that they had gone out to get some tacos and there it was. Is that a pot story or what? So I helped them get the couch inside and they moved out a few weeks later. I'm guessing they actually got kicked out because of the smell. They were good guys though.

I moved at the start of 2010 up near UCLA. I had donated platelets there many times and I like the area. I checked the rent; it was significantly lower. The place was loaded with co-eds and everything was within walking distance. So I made the move. I found a place by accident; the landlady was amazed that I came in when I did. She said that I had saved her, and we became almost instant friends. She was this little Persian lady who was sweet as can be. She gave me a great deal on the place and I moved in fast with the help of my parents. The apartment itself wasn't bad aside from the sink backing up every so often and the water sometimes coming out of the tap with a yellow tint to it. I decided not to worry, I had a filter.

The guys that lived next door to me were terrible. They would invite some really skanky and obnoxious girls over and have loud—I will call them parties—at night. They had a dog that left his little doggy presents everywhere and they never cleaned up after him. Fleas were everywhere; I know because I got attacked one night by the little blood suckers. I and several other people eventually had enough and we got them evicted.

I also learned something about UCLA that I didn't know before. There is a tradition every quarter during finals' week called the Midnight Yell. During this time at the stroke midnight students will yell at the top of their lungs to release stress. Sounds like a good idea right? Except for one thing, if you don't know that it's coming then it sits you straight up in bed. The first scream that I heard came from a girl, and it was blood curdling. I thought somebody was being murdered. I jumped out of bed and grabbed my baseball bat. Then I heard a guy scream and another girl and another guy. I was very confused. It took a while, but I eventually got used to the thing and I developed the only defense—stay up till midnight, let them scream and then go to bed.

In August 2010, I got the chance to get a new place upstairs. At the time I was living on the ground floor. It felt more like a cave than an apartment. There was very little light even in the day and that was starting to wear on my mood. So over the space of 2 days I moved myself up 3 floors to my new place directly above where I was living. That was hard work. I managed to do everything myself with the exception of my couch. I was using the elevator to do most of the heavy lifting for me, but when I loaded the couch in the elevator stopped and locked. I was trapped in a box about 4X5X9 with my couch. So I did what any sensible person would do—I screamed and yelled until help came. Are you nuts? I'm not going to sit and wait for somebody to realize that I'm stuck somewhere while both my apartments are unlocked and my stuff is not secured. The guys that helped me out and helped me carry my couch up the stairs thought I had panicked. They were wrong. I just know that if you are stuck make as much noise as you can until help arrives.

Let's rewind a bit to the previous summer.

As I started to settle into my new village I made new friends. I was amazed at how open people were. This was very evident at the retreat. Every year Emperor's College offers a class called the retreat. About 60 students drive up to a cabin in Big Bear for the weekend. There are team building exercises, meditation and a great time for all. I loved it. I got to meet the founder of the school, BDK as he is known. I even got to meditate with him. He is one of the three wisest men that

I have ever met. The first was a Benedictine monk that taught me about Heaven. The second was C. B. who taught me how to meditate.

The following week I started my first shift in the herbal pharmacy at the school. This was lab class and a requirement for my education. The first person I met was K. J. She was a beautiful blonde with an A-frame hair cut and brown eyes with specks of yellow throughout them. I thought she was an intern, I had no idea she was just another student that happened to be at work that day. She spoke with an accent that I recognized to be Israeli, from the Tel Aviv region. I asked her where she was from—my guess was correct. For the next few weeks, she among a few other people were my bosses, and I had a great time. I can't say that I learned a lot, but what I did learn was important.

A few weeks after my last lab shift, I got a phone call early in the morning from K. J. She was exasperated, and needed my help. I rushed down to the clinic, and I was offered a job. What had happened was one of the people that worked in the lab quit without notice, and left everyone there in trouble. I filled the position very well, especially without a lot of experience. K. J. and I started to spend a lot of time together, and something embarrassing happened. I developed a crush on this woman.

In my defense, she was very beautiful, very intelligent, very strong and very kind. Who could ask for more? I actually thought that she liked me as more than just a colleague or a friend, because she was nice to me and treated me like a person and not like a wild animal or a machine. I was very used to women not speaking to men unless it was absolutely necessary, because that is how things are done in Utah. Basically, if a woman talks to you, kisses you on the cheek and treats you like a person she wants to either date you, sleep with you or marry you. K. J. did not come from that culture. She was raised that you kiss your friends on the cheek, and actually talk to people you work with outside of work even if they are male.

During this half way romance. I committed the worst sin a psychic can commit. I read someone without her consent. While K. J. was on holiday in Washington, I overheard a very worried conversation between G. B. and BDK. I asked what was going on when they had finished, there was a problem with the health of a family member. I wanted to help, so I offered to read her and this family member. She didn't know what I was doing and I did it anyway. I told her that if this was not resolved soon that in 3 years this family member would be dead. G. B. cried, and I instantly knew that I had done something wrong. I tried to apologize but she would not hear me.

When K. J. got back, she pulled me aside and told me what I had done wrong and that I needed to fix it or I would be in more trouble. That day I went before G. B. and I knelt before her, which was not easy for me to do because of my bad knees. I told her that I had sinned against her and that I was sorry. I offered her the opportunity to hit me, cut me, take money or property as recompense. She said it was unnecessary, and that I was forgiven. That was the worst sin that I have ever committed and I promised then as I do now that I will never do that ever again.

This was a sin because reading someone without their consent is a violation of trust. At least it is like reading somebody's mail. At worst it is a form of rape. If you are psychic and you are reading people just to read them STOP DOING THAT NOW YOU ARE IN HUGE VIOLATION. If you ever get read by a person and you did not permit them to do so, please tell them to stop and please be firm about your privacy.

I made my feelings known to K. J. a few months after we had met. I had to do it, holding it in like I had been taught was driving me insane. She told me that she was going through some emotional purification, and wasn't ready or even capable of any kind of relationship. So I agreed to wait for her to get better. That summer she seemed to be doing better, so I asked her out. She said that she did love me, but more like a brother and that she was going back to her old boyfriend. I wasn't as heartbroken as you might think. I wasn't even angry. I felt like the matter had finally been resolved, because I had decided that no matter the outcome I would be happy with it even if it was not what I wanted.

It was around this time that I sang in a karaoke bar. I wrote earlier that because of what performing means in Utah I refuse to sing unless I'm drunk, this was no exception. As part of a company outing the entire staff gets taken out by the founder of Emperor's as a thank you for all our hard work. At the end of dinner, we as a staff decided to go out for drinks and singing. The first place we stopped at was all in Korean, so none of us knew what to do. We then went to a second place down the street. I was amazed at how much of a dive it was, but when in Rome. I ordered myself a beer and we sat down to listen to some actually good music being sung fairly well. I will confess I am a bit of a lightweight, so after my social beer I was having a great time. I decided to sing for my friends I put my name and song down and handed it to the DJ. An hour later I went up on stage. The alcohol had actually run through my system, and I was stone-cold sober. I figured that I would be a coward if I backed out so I belted out *Witchy Woman* to the best of my ability. I sucked just like I knew I would, but nobody seemed to care. You see in Utah there are no such things as karaoke bars, hell there are barely any bars to begin with. That is not to say that I have never done karaoke before, I had actually been booed off the stage when I sang with my friends by some of my friends. But in LA I was allowed to sing and not be good at it. It was one of the most amazing experiences that I have ever had.

The summer of 2010 was a little hard on me to say the least. I told a woman that I had feelings for her and I sang on stage for the first time without getting booed off. That August would test me in a way that I never would have figured.

Once a year in San Diego there is a convention that many people call "Nerdy Gras"; I was extremely curious so I paid the $20 fee and got my ticket. I went down on the last day which was a Sunday and I expected to have an okay time. This is what happened.

I left home at about 5 AM so I could get there by 7 AM. The drive was longer than I had expected, but I managed it. I actually enjoy San Diego and I don't mind driving long distances. I found a parking spot and went over to the convention center. There was a line full of people wrapping around the building. Many were dressed up mostly as comic book characters, but I saw a few from some sci-fi shows and some Japanese Anime characters. The first line that I chose was for the people that were part of the convention. I don't know if you have ever been to one of these things, but the people that are paid to help you out have absolutely no communication skills what so ever. After standing there for about 30 minutes I was finally told that I was standing in the wrong line and I had to go around the building to get into the right line. It took me asking 5 different people to get this information in plain English. So I ran around and found my place about 3 blocks away. I was now very grumpy. Every single dorky conversation that I heard grated my nerves. About an hour later I finally got in and got my ID badge.

I figured that everything was fine so I went into the convention hall itself to perhaps find some food; nothing was open. Nobody was there, not even the people running the displays. So I left the convention center to find something to eat. There was only one thing open at that time which was about 8 AM. It was a restaurant inspired by the science fiction channel. I thought it was a good place so I sat down. I got my menu and looked it over. The cheapest thing was biscuits and gravy at $20 and orange juice for 5 bucks. I figured why not; this was the only place open and I didn't feel like wandering through bum infested territory with my stomach growling. Breakfast sucked. Had it only cost $5 it would have been fine. But $25?! Really?!

After breakfast I went back to the convention center, and I found my way to the actual convention.

That is, the people that were selling a bunch of nerd stuff were finally around. The place was packed. It was like being in a room that was the size of an entire football stadium brimming with clones of W. R. The longer I spent there the angrier I got. These people were having the time of their life over nothing. Everything was so expensive. I got fee comics shoved in my face everywhere I went. I do not like comics, at all. This made me angrier. I managed to last about 2 hours in that place just wandering around. I couldn't take it anymore so I left. As I crossed the train tracks that run beside the convention center I dumped all the free stuff in a sidewalk garbage can and I went back to my car. I swore then and there that I will never go to another of those things again. If I do, it will be under the invite of an exceptionally beautiful woman that can take the sting of the experience out, and we had better have a suite. Otherwise I ain't going.

The ride home was chore. I was beat from the ordeal. As I was leaving San Diego, I realized I was falling asleep so I pulled off to the side of the road and took a half restful nap. I got home sometime in the afternoon, and I went immediately to bed. A phone call from Mom woke me up, and I was cranky. I told her what I had done that morning. She only laughed, and asked if I had learned anything.

About a month after the thing with K. J. happened something very odd happened in my mind. Over the years I had developed strategies for dealing with emotions. I believed myself to be in complete control to the point that I could turn my emotions on and off like a light switch or a faucet. I lost control. I started to become paranoid and withdrawn. I thought that everybody was laughing at me and treating me like I was stupid and that they were out to get me. I knew that wasn't the case, I had no basis for these beliefs but they were there just the same so I sought treatment from the school's clinic. One of my co-workers, G. B., managed to stabilize me, and get my mind to a point where I could reason properly again. BDK noticed that my mind was different now. I was ordered to go on sabbatical for the quarter and to concentrate on my studies. I agreed and thus began one of the most intense and amazing journeys of my life.

I started off with meditation. I had done something similar to this all my life. I was very used to going into my mind, locating the offending impulse or emotion and destroying it. So I did the same thing as before, the problem was for everything that I did it refused to fall away and continued to persist. When I got rid of an emotion or an urge, it would just come back. I eventually got fed up with the idea of spinning my wheels, and I gathered up my entire personality. I packed it into a little ball inside my mind and I destroyed it in a huge explosion.

The resulting manifestation in my meditative mind was a post-apocalyptic wasteland. There were fires and charred trees and black clouds in the sky. Then I said, "Reset," and the wasteland was replaced by a small forest and the worksite of a mansion under construction. There were workmen running around moving wood and stone and putting things together. I found the foreman, and asked what all this was. He looked at me and said that it was me. I could tell that I had a lot of work to do.

So over the next day and a half I witnessed as the house began to be built. As it was being built, I located basic parts of my personality such as my intellect, my humor, my prowess with various subjects. The rest of me I had to find.

I realized that I would need help so I went down to the school's clinic, and I got an appointment with BDK, he agreed to help me. He warned me that it would not be easy, and it would be very painful. I wasn't scared. He told me to remove my shirt and lie down on my stomach. K. J and G. B were in the room with us assisting BDK. He took out a tool called a lance. It is about 5 inches long with the last inch being a very long and thick needle. He then took this tool and poked me in the back and scalp in very select spots. He was trying to make me bleed, and yes it hurt like hell. It hurt so bad that I actually growled in pain, but I knew and understood what he was doing. Over the next several weeks I went in and had this procedure done once a week like clockwork. The pain was intense. After the bleeding I was turned over on my back and acupuncture needles were placed in my abdomen or hands and feet. I was so light-headed from pain and the minor loss of blood which was only about a teaspoon worth. I started taking regular herbs in a powder form. I actually credit these treatments with making my meditations so effective. Had I done the work by myself, I would have still been building the house, 5 months after I started.

I started to search in the forest for various aspects of my personality. I was amazed at what I had found. For instance, I ran into a part of my personality that was a feral beast boy. In the past when I had encountered this thing I would kill it. This time I decided to absorb it, he stayed absorbed. I next encountered a version of me that was a vampire. I did the same thing and absorbed him. As grotesque as these versions of me might seem, they are actually aspects of my personality. The feral one represents my instincts and my willingness to fight for survival. The vampire represents my tenacity, and my ability to somehow skirt death.

There were so many that I found; too many for me to tell you about, but here are a few: a soldier, a monk, a guy dressed in a fantastic suit, an artist, an actor and each one of the 13 elements.

That part was intense. I had to absorb all of the elements independently, and they did not want to go peacefully. Not all of my personality characteristics that I found wanted to go peacefully either. Some of the aspects I actually had to battle or chase down. Some of those battles especially the ones with the elements got very violent. The violence involved in their assimilation into my personality is actually symbolic of the damage that was done to my personality by various people and groups and ways of thought. After about a week of daily meditation the house was completed and filled with aspects of my personality.

When that was done I looked around in my mind and tried to experience the environment. I discovered a red rock cliff that rose up above the trees in the forest. I touched the rock wall and said, “peace.” It began to lower. I lowered about 30 cubic feet of rock that day, and a lot more remained. So I took to the air and soared above the cliff and the trees. What I discovered stunned me.

The cliff was actually the edge of a huge plateau. Although the rock was red on the forest side, on the top of the plateau, the rock was black. Set in a seemingly random pattern were large bonfires, with the largest of them in the center of the mass. Dark black clouds swirled in the sky while a beautiful blue sky existed above the house. I had no idea what to do. So I sat down on the edge of the plateau and spoke the word peace, this made the rocks lower and fall. I could only lower 30 square feet of rock at a time per day. This continued for about a week. The method was little better than putting a house fire out by spitting on it. I asked for help from BDK and he set is needles in me. When I meditated again, most of the rocks had fallen away leaving only the fires and walkways between them.

I thought, "What should I do about this?" So I went over to the largest of the fires and I sat in the middle of it. I knew the fire wouldn't burn me; the fire is only a symbol. I tried to extinguish the flames, but they would go no lower. Then I added peace to the flames and they grew taller and brighter. The fire grew with intensity until it became a column of white light. It shot up into the sky and broke through the black clouds. I realized what the fire/column of light was—it was my soul. It seemed that I had diminished the expression of my soul by trying to be a "good boy" and bend to everyone's expectations of me. I then started to go around to each of the smaller fires. I found walking around them or near them were people that looked a bit like me. I knew these weren't aspects of my personality; I had already dealt with and assimilated those. If the big fire was me, then the smaller fires had to be past versions of me, and the people walking around the fires were my past incarnations. I found many of the ones that I already knew about like the pirate and the sculptor. Over the next week and a half I absorbed each of the people. Some were more willing than others. Then after I absorbed the person, I sat in the fire and turned it into a column of light. I then took that column of light and added it to the large one in the center of the plateau. With each fire I added, the big one grew and grew.

At most I could do five in a day. I got a massive headache after each session, but I knew that I needed to do this. As the large column continued to grow, it began to change. When I was nearly finished, the large column began to throw off sparks. Initially I tried to stop it from doing so until I sampled one of the sparks. I held the spark in my hand and all that I felt was negative energy. The column was throwing off all the negativity that I had picked up not only in this life but all my past lives combined. So I went back to work of adding in the fires. When the last of the fires was added, the column changed again. It was now several times the size of the original form and now had lightning coursing around it. It was the most spectacular image that my mind has ever spawned. Imagine if you will a column of bright white light with the diameter of a large house and tall enough to be of imperceptible height and to have long chains of lightning wrapping around it in crisscross patterns.

I thought there was only one thing left to do now. I entered the light and sat inside of it. I said, "Merge house," and the whole thing slowly lifted off and moved toward the house. I had no idea what to expect. I thought that both could be annihilated or perhaps just one. What happened surpassed my expectations. The house and the column merged seamlessly. Now when I meditate and enter the house as it sits on a half lit half dark tiny rocky ball, I see all the different aspects of my personality living inside in harmony along with huge currents of electricity running throughout the house. I am truly proud of my accomplishment of unifying both the past and present aspects of my personality.

I honestly thought that I was done. I thought that the only thing left to do was to rebuild, which I figured the needles would do for me. I did continue to meditate, and when urges came up I did what I had learned to do and that is to allow them to exist but in the capacity that I set for them. For example, I knew that I had lustful thoughts of many women that I know and have seen with the country star excluded. I went into meditation and I routed out all those thoughts and feelings by turning the women to ash during the purification. If my feelings for them were in nature pure, say for K. J., they would then turn back into the women that I knew and loved. Minor meditations like this continued until something very odd happened.

I was a tutor for biology in my school. One day as I was tutoring a friend of mine, things stopped making sense to me. As I have said, when I see the future I don't see certainty I see possibility. I had gotten a treatment that morning, and I felt fine, but as I started to teach this girl my perception of reality began to warp. I remember I was standing at the front of the classroom and she was sitting in 2 places at once holding the same pen in 2 different hands and asking me many questions all at the same time. Many times I had to ask her to repeat her question, so I could tell which one was actually the real question. I looked around and saw so many things that could all have actually happened. I could not tell which one was real, and it was giving me a huge headache. It was so bad that I had to stop several times to order my thoughts and make sure I was where I thought I was. As I continued to teach the feeling got worse so I pushed and got through as much as I could. My student asked if I was okay, at least I think she did, and I said I just wasn't feeling well.

After I finished teaching I called K. J. to get help. She advised me to get into the sunlight and meditate while breathing slowly. I managed to stabilize myself so I could drive home; not being able to tell the difference of what car is in front of you is a bad thing. When I got home I jumped into meditation and I realized what had happened.

The treatment that I had received that day had removed something very large from me. In the meditation I was shown a tapestry with a large hole in it. I scanned the hole and the image of the Salt Lake Mormon Temple phased in and out. The influence of the Church was gone! All that was there was tattered remains, so I filled the hole with my new spiritual system. This is still very new at the time I write this, so I have no idea what will happen with it.

After I got out of the meditation I called K. J., and asked her to ask me a question about the Church. I was testing to see if I had an emotional reaction with the question. I did not have one. She at first did not understand what had happened until I explained it to her.

From then on I knew things were going to be very different.

I realized a few days later that this had happened before. In a lesser capacity during high school and college I would lapse through various levels of reality and assume possibilities were realities. Like Gore won the election, or the Iraq War never happened, etc. My friends back then realized what was happening to me and they would mess with me by making stuff up and saying that it actually happened.

I know some of you think I'm insane for saying this, but it makes sense in quantum mechanics. In physics there is a law that says if it can happen then it must happen. If however 2 events are mutually exclusive then how can they both happen? They occur in different versions of the same reality. This is the basis for the idea of multiple universes. So there are Earths where I never moved to California, or I did move but I moved there as a kid when my dad got the job offer in Orange County. There are Earths where the Nazis won World War II; there are also Earths where the war was never fought because Hitler wasn't born. The variations are literally infinite and they are based on the various possibilities of every event in the flow of history.

The event that occurred in the classroom opened up an entire new level of treatment for BDK to do with me. Because the Church was now gone from my energetic make up I had to relearn how to function. I didn't have anything to hate anymore, so as a result my emotions became unpredictable. You would think that not hating is a good thing, and it is. The problem arises when the change happens too quickly. The damage became evident a few weeks later.

After I got my job back in the pharmacy, I discovered that things had changed in the time that I had been away. I made the assumption that things were the same as when I had left. I was wrong. I made several mistakes on my first day of work. One of my coworkers who was now effectively above me called me up and I thought she yelled at me. The way she did it angered me, but I allowed it to pass. The next week, after a large staff meeting I spoke to her and I volunteered to fix up the inventory of the various herbal medicines that were sold by our pharmacy. She said sure. So the next day I came in on my day off and I got to work. The place was a mess. I localized all the medicines and I counted the units; this is what is done as standard procedure during inventory. The person that I had asked if I could do this had only been doing a cursory glance at the medicines once a week just to see what we were running out of. I fixed up and cataloged the entire supply. I came in at about 8 AM and I left at 3 PM. The person that I had asked if I could do this yelled at me, at least that is what I took it as. I thought she had called me stupid, by saying that everything that I had done was no good, and that she would have to take time out of her day and do everything again. I told K. J. what had happened. This person was ordered to apologize to me, which she did the next day. What I heard her say was something completely different. I heard her say that everything was my fault and I had to apologize to her for over stepping my bounds and making her look stupid. In reality she did not say this; this is what I had heard.

I screamed at her. She had hit a button in me that I didn't know existed. I tried to stop myself but I couldn't do it. I was so angry that I had gone insane. I felt like everyone was against me, and that they all thought I was an idiot; exactly the way I felt as a kid. A few days later, K. J. and I spoke. I was given the true sequence of events, and I realized the problem was me. I was taken off of active duty again, and ordered to seek treatment. I felt terrible. I adopted the idea that until proven otherwise I was to be thought of as insane, and that I should simply do the opposite of my natural urge.

BDK understood what had happened, and he said that it was actually a good thing. We began to focus on a very specific aspect of my physiology. I only know how to explain this in Chinese medical terms, please bare with me. Everyone has emotions. How we do or do not use them can influence how we manifest a disease, especially mental ones. I was taught to not use my emotions; my mother and the Church told me that they were dangerous and should never be used. The blood stores emotion in Chinese medicine; this is because of the idea that emotions are a manifestation of the personality which has links with the blood itself; the idea is an entire chapter in my text book there is not enough space for me here to explain it. The Liver, which is different from the liver in western medicine, stores blood. So, by the transitive property, the Liver stores emotion.

BDK already knew this and he had been treating my Liver this whole time with the bleeding and the herbs and the various other needles that he was putting in me. Now that I understood what was happening, I began to do a very focused meditation. I entered meditation and instead of going into my personality I went into my Liver. The way my mind chose to display the organ was very interesting.

In Chinese medicine, the Liver is made of Wood. My mind chose to represent the Liver as being a forest. The forest was dark, and seemed to be very toxic. The trees were almost leafless even though the trees seemed to be very thick and healthy. The streams and rivers that ran through the forest were almost black and stagnant. The place reeked of decaying and rotting wood. This was a very bad sign. As I walked through the forest I was attacked by a very large, red, hairless dog/wolf. This was the embodiment of rage that my mind had chosen. I knew I couldn't absorb the beast, so I grabbed the thing and pushed the exact inverse of rage into it. I used kindness instead of love, and the beast rotted away and turned to ash. I was next attacked by hate in the form of a yeti. I did something similar. I found emotions pertaining mostly to sins like lust in the form of a little fat guy that wanted to hump everything, greed looked like a greasy businessman, and depression/sloth was self destructive person that was a cutter. There were a lot of them, and it took me a few days to clean out the forest. It was surprisingly difficult and I had to think on my feet as to what emotion would counter act the issue. Many were counterintuitive, and as a result I had to do this on a bit of trial and error basis. If you ever find yourself in the situation that I have with trying to purify your mind and emotions please use somebody that has good and reputable training and has the skill to help you through. Do not under any circumstances, do this on your own.

As I removed the negative emotions from my Liver, the forest began to look better. The trees seemed to come to life again. Leaves grew on the branches and the smell of decay left the air. The forest got brighter, and the streams started to move with cleaner water. It took me a while to do this. As stressful as it was, it was actually kind of fun. I also figured out the cause of the disease. It had to do with the way that I was perceiving time. I didn't necessarily see time as the beginning, middle and end that everyone else does. For me everything was now. That means, not only am I at this moment twenty-seven, I am also nineteen and forty-five. The day that I entered kindergarten is the same day that I graduated from college. As a result of this all the trauma that I experienced as a kid and a teenager I was reliving in some fashion on a daily basis. This caused an immense amount of emotional stagnation. Since emotions are stored in the Liver, and the Liver does not like stagnation, the madness that I experienced was only a matter of time…so to speak.

Many people that I have told this to think that being able to experience time in a non-linear fashion would be kind of neat. I disagree. I was not always able to do this, and I had to unlearn how to do it. And no, I did not pick this up from some stupid comic book. Not being able to distinguish between past, present and future and different possibilities is very stressful, because my human brain is actually not wired to be able to cope with it. And never mind that nonsense about how we only use 10 percent of our brains. If that was our natural level, we would even have the other ninety. Nature would consider that to be a waste and it would be gone. How effectively you use that brain matter is something else entirely. Not to mention, just because you can do something does not mean that you should do something.

When I was dating D. E., she made me promise that I would do one thing that I had never done on my birthday for my birthday. For my birthday after we dated, I went to Disneyland for free. I went with my parents and we had a great time. I technically kept the promise the following year. One of my friends from school invited me out to a house she was sitting for a party. I jumped at the chance because I was certain that my birthday would be a non-event. I drove up with a bottle of whiskey, because it is rude to show up empty handed. I was the only one that drank from my bottle; everyone else preferred vodka. I got good and liquored and I decided that I wasn't going home, so I continued to drink. I switched to vodka mostly because that's what was put in front of me. Then after midnight on my actual birthday we toasted with champaigne. I actually don't like champagne, but I was completely drunk and didn't care. I was then shown to my bed by my friend and I started to drift off to sleep.

An upset stomach woke me up I tried to quell it, but I failed. I burped and I watched the entire night of food and drink came up and onto my shirt. I tried to run to the bathroom to find a toilet; I puked the whole way there. I managed to get some of the mess in the bowl but the damage was done. I did my best to clean some of it up, but I couldn't see much. I was covered in my own vomit, and I was exhausted. The good news is I was no longer drunk; I had puked up most of the alcohol. My head was clear but I was freaking out. I attempted to sleep in my car, but I soon realized that it wouldn't work, so I drove home.

I felt guilty the whole way. I got home and jumped in the shower, and did some laundry. When I woke up a few hours later I felt like crap. I had a hangover, and I was ashamed. I called my friend to apologize, she seemed to accept it but we would not talk again for several months afterward as part of my punishment for puking and running. As a result my 27th birthday was rather quiet, just as I had figured it would be, with the added bonus of guilt and a hangover. As long as I live I will never do that again.

In January of 2011 I became the member of the Emperor's College Student Council in charge of tutorials. I'm really no good at politics, but I am good at teaching and at getting people the help that they need. Currently as I write this, the office is going well as stressful as it is.

For the most part my life is just trying to survive graduate school. This is not easy, and each successive class adds more information and more difficulty. In March 2011, I was finally at a level where I need to pass a test called the Mid-curriculum Exam. It is a 4 hour, 200 question battery that is based on all the information we learn in the program in the first 2 years. On average students take the test 3 times before they are able to successfully pass it. It is the gate keeper to the internship and the continuance in the program. I was able to pass the test at the end of spring on my third try.

One of the biggest reasons I was able to pass was because I had decided to move from my place in Westwood to a different place in the Valley. I was tired of the noise and the filth that I was living in. My water came out of the tap yellow for five minutes! That is not sanitary at all. Cockroaches regularly crawled across my feet while I was studying. My neighbors were obnoxious as hell and they tended to be up at all hours of the night because mommy and daddy weren't around to tell them to brush their teeth and go to bed because they had school in the morning.

I really needed to pass the Mid-curriculum, so I asked my land-lady to sublet my place and I took off. I found a place on the border of Sherman Oaks and Van Nuys and I moved myself…again. But this time I had some help from some friends as sparing as it was. I was loaned a pick-up and my next door neighbor from Westwood helped me with the couch.

I was so glad to be out. The new apartment was cleaner, cheaper and it felt safer. The people that lived there were actually nice to me and actually greeted me in the morning with a friendly hello. The kids in Westwood never did this; in fact I think they were scared of me for some strange reason.

That June just after my move to the Valley, I was given the opportunity to go to a place that I had wanted to visit ever since I learned of its existence—The Playboy Mansion. At one time I had a subscription to the magazine. As a perk of that subscription I was given special access to certain things like first releases of sunglasses and various other items. I was also given access to special groupons for things like dinners at nice restaurants. It was through these groupons that I got to go to the mansion. Usually the price to get into the party is $1000—$10,000 if you want to sit down somewhere with bottle service. This groupon got me into the party for $700! I figured it was a once in a lifetime chance so I took it. I was very excited; I told all of my friends at school where I was going. The banging sound I heard was their jaws hitting the floor.

So the night came and I went to the party. It was nothing like I had anticipated. We were bused in from a parking garage a couple of miles away. When I signed my name on the registry the woman there commented on my signature and asked if I was a doctor. I said I was. Come on, what was I going to do, disagree with her? After I got on the bus, three very obnoxious guys sat next to me. They were pick-up artists. The whole time all that they did was talk about all the girls that they had hooked up with in the past few days. They exchanged pictures of these girls and rated them on a scale of 1 to 10 with 10 being perfect. I wondered then if the whole night was going to be like those guys.

After I left the bus, I did my best to get away from those guys and try to have a good time. I moved through this large pink circus tent, there were painted ladies everywhere. A painted lady is a woman who is wearing only body paint and nothing else. I got some pictures with a few of those girls. I thought they were beautiful, but not my type sadly. I left the tent and I started to look for food. Dinner was going to be served in a few minutes so I continued to look around. I made my way to the grotto where I followed these 2 very lovely ladies in. Actual entry into the grotto was difficult for me however. The smell of the place was vile. It reeked of emotions like lust and shame. I got 2 inches inside the door and I turned around.

I then got myself a drink and something to eat. The food was actually very good. Among the usual finger food items were beef kabob and mini lamb burgers. If nothing else I would at least have eaten well. After I ate, I looked for a place to sit down. I found one on the other side of the grotto's outer pool.

As I sat there drinking the last of my jack on the rocks, a very large black man sat down next to me. He seemed to not be doing well. I actually thought he was tripping out, and that I might have to intervene on his behalf. When he realized I was talking to him, he said he just had a headache because he was exhausted due to long hours of teaching golf. I asked why he was there, and he said that his wife was a close friend of Hef's. I asked him if I could help him out with his problem—I was an acupuncturist. He said sure. So I did a couple of points on his head and some on his hands and legs with my fingernails. He said he felt better afterward, so I told him to go home and rest for about 10 hours and he should be fine. I hope he took my advice.

I went back into the crowd, and I started to feel nauseated from the smell. What I smelled was not body odors; it was emotions like shame, lust, fear and greed among other such lovely emotions. The more people that arrived the worse the smell got. I reached out via a text to a close friend of mine, and I relayed my experience to her. She asked me if it smelled like home or if it smelled foul. It smelled foul. She advised me to be strong and to get out of there as soon as I could. I decided that I needed to leave, but the night was still young and I wanted to get my money's worth. So I walked around the grounds.

I managed to find my way to the zoo, where I met a beautiful white cockatiel named Chloe. When Chloe was first set on my arm, her crest flared up and her wings opened a little. That is a sign that a bird makes to warn the other animal not to mess with the bird. I told her that it was okay and I just smelled like a cat. She calmed down immediately. I petted her and I had a couple of pictures taken with her. She even smiled for me.

I left the party soon afterward. On my way home from the party I came to a realization. For about 4 hours I had been surrounded by some of the most beautiful women in the world, yet my thoughts were only for one person in particular and I had reached out to her earlier that night. I realized I was in love with that woman, and I was going to devote myself to becoming worthy of her. It took my spending $700 to go to a party in Beverly Hills and being disgusted by it to realize my true feelings for her. I'm sure you would love to know who it is. Out of respect however, I have decided to not name her. She does however know how I feel, and that is good enough for us.

As I continued my purification process, I moved through my body and I sought out all the bad things that I could so I could help myself. After I finished my Liver, I went into my Kidney. In the Chinese System, the Kidney is made of water, so when I entered it my mind chose to display it as a vast ocean with a small island about 5 feet wide for me to stand on. The first time I entered the Kidney I stood on the island and I listened to the gentle sloshing of the waves. Then I heard someone call me a loser. Then I heard a similar voice say, "pathetic."

I looked down into the water and I saw a bunch of eels circling my island and whispering very negative things around me. I yelled out and told them to stop. They just laughed. So I reached into the surf and grabbed one of them. I ripped the eel from the water and smacked it onto a table that I had I had created. I killed it with the smack and then I turned it to ash and it blew away. Over the next 2 hours of meditation I continued to do this until every eel was gone. I told BDK about it the next day, he was very impressed. He said that they were "evil qi" that I had picked up years ago and fostered due to my ignorance.

After the eels, I dove into the ocean of my Kidney, and I found something very odd. There were little to no animals living in the water. Mostly what I found were predators like sharks and barracuda or tuna. There was nothing else. I swam deeper all the while enjoying the fact that I could breathe under water. I reached the ocean floor and discovered that it was littered with corpses of whales and various other creatures in various stages of decomposition. I was not sure what they represented, but I reached out and purified one anyway. As it turned to dust I was hit with a memory of a fight that I was in as a kid. The corpses were manifestations of my bad memories, while the living animals were manifestations of my good memories.

Over the next few days or perhaps weeks, it became difficult to tell, I got rid of hundreds of these corpses. The more corpses that I removed the better and lighter I felt. Also the more I did, the more living animals started to appear in the water. I eventually got strong enough to simply reach into the ocean and purify the whole thing in one grand move. When I did this the water lit up and bubbled. After I felt that it was done I jumped in and started down to the bottom again. On the way down to the bottom, I found my ocean to be teaming with life of all kinds from coral to large schools of fish. On the bottom of the ocean I found that it was devoid of corpses. My mission there was completed.

From my Kidney I went into my Heart. In Chinese Medicine, the Heart is not just a pump that moves blood; it is the house of the mind and the expression of who you are not just to yourself, but to the world as well. When I entered my Heart, I found a beautiful palace with 6 spires wrapped around a central tower. Each spire and the central tower had a large and very beautiful rose window. Around the palace there stood a large stone wall with thick iron spikes and a wrought iron gate.

I approached the gate and attempted to open it. A voice called out from the palace, "Who goes there?"

I replied, "I am Richard owner of this palace."

"It has been a long time since you have been here. Please come in."

The gate opened and I stepped inside. Between the gate and the palace there was a vast rose garden full of red rose bushes in various states of bloom. I stopped on the path to the main door of the palace, and I knelt down. I touched the pathway and I started to purify it. The gate that I had just walked through turned to gold and some of the roses turned white. I goal was just to test area and see if worked needed to me done—it did. I entered the palace and I found that it was far too simple.

There were 7 terraces each leading up to the spires. Each terrace had 7 wooden doors with iron hinges spaced out evenly. The palace itself was made of blocks of a brownish rock that was rather non-descript.

I immediately went to work, and over the next couple of weeks I turned the brown rock into beautiful ruby quartz. I went into each of the doors on each of the levels and I routed out all of the negative and less than positive things that I was currently using like my impressions on women, society, education, money etc. As I got stronger, and I purified more things in my Heart I started to have bouts of depression. I kept thinking that I had no friends, and that I would always be alone. I forced myself to stop thinking this because I knew that this was just the "evil qi" trying to survive my attacks.

After I had completed all that I could in my Heart I went outside to the wall. I decided that it was no longer was good enough, so I changed it. I got rid of the stone and the iron and the gold and instead I put up an energy field that was selectively permeable. As I was changing the wall I noticed that stuck on the iron spikes were what looked like ghosts. When I examined them I realized that they were emotions and ideas from other people that I had picked up. The ones that I managed to keep from getting in were caught on the spikes and seemed to be rotting there. This was in fact part of my depression. The energy field that I erected allows for good things like love or kindness to pass freely through. It prevents negative things like anger and hate from ever touching me. However, I allow it to release all my emotions when they come up to prevent a buildup.

From the Heart I moved into the Lung. In this organ I found a great factory with about two dozen smoke stacks spewing either white or black smoke. The stacks that had the white smoke were made out of metal, while the stacks with black smoke were made out of bricks. I identified the problem as the brick stacks. In Chinese Medicine the Lung is made metal. Even though earth feeds metal its place is down in the Spleen—the digestive system—which to me is a vast red rock desert similar to Moab, Utah. If there is a lot of earth in the Lung that means the Lung is not functioning properly. This malfunction in me consisted of anxiety, especially with personal interaction. So I set to work of changing the brick smoke stacks to metal. I expected that I would be just fine, I was wrong.

I got so sick. I picked up a cough that would not go away no matter what I did to it. I even lost my voice for 2 days. I realized soon that the issue was internal, and as a result I needed to continue with my personal purification. I was told that I would have to change my exercise regimen to include my old *aikitaiso* from aikido to get my voice back. Everything was fine with the exception of the persistent cough and gurgling water sound in my throat. I finally managed to kick it with the help of K. J. in late October.

I mentioned the cough because I actually wasn't sick. The anti-viral and anti-bacterial therapies were ineffective. The problem was emotional. I was having a respiratory condition because I was holding some emotions in my lungs effectively. So, as I was expelling these emotions from my lungs it would make perfect sense that I would get a cough. As soon as I finished dealing with those emotions, the cough went away.

The previous August in my techniques class, something very bad happened to me. We were learning a technique called cupping. In this technique a glass jar in the shape of a ball is placed on the back of the patient with the help of suction induced by a burning cotton ball coated with rubbing alcohol. Normally this is a very safe and very effective procedure with only good things happening and the worse being a circular bruise forming where the cup was placed.

This would not be the case with me that night. My partner prepped her tools for the cupping procedure that she was going to do on me. She grabbed 2 cotton balls, instead of just one and she soaked them in alcohol and wrung them out just as she had been taught. She did not get enough of the alcohol, because on the second cup she attempted to place on me she missed and hit the lip of the cup. Flaming drops of 99 percent alcohol squirted out of the cotton and onto my back. That is not supposed to happen.

At first I didn't realize what was happening. I felt hot and that was it. Then the heat started to increase. I put two and two together and I realized I was on fire. I screamed for help and my teacher tackled me with a towel to snuff out the flames. By the time the fire was out I had been on fire for about 1 minute. The result was second degree burns to my neck and shoulder on my right side.

The burn cream that I used that night was based in sesame oil, so I smelled like dinner all night while I tried to sleep. That was disturbing. When I first noticed it, I was trying to sleep on the couch—my bed was out as a possibility. I kept smelling fried chicken, and it was making me hungry. It took about a week for my wounds to heal due to my natural healing ability, topical burn cream, herbs and energetic work performed by a dear friend at school. Currently I have second degree burn scars on my body, and I am proud to show them.

The student that accidently burned me felt terrible; she called me 3 times that weekend to see if I was okay. Everybody expected me to sue her and make her life a living hell. Why should I do that? She made a mistake. I was actually glad that it happened to me, and not to somebody who would sue. I told everybody at school to pay attention to what they're doing when they do cupping, and then my burns would be an isolated incident.

Amazingly as my burns were healing, I was happy. I was smiling and cheerful and joking around with my friends. No one could understand why I was like this. The reason is where the burns were. In Chinese Medicine around the neck there exists a special series of points called the Windows of the Sky. These points are used to release long term illnesses and emotional patterns that are pathological. In a way I inadvertently fought fire with fire. By being burned I was forced to release my old emotions and embrace a new way of acting—being happy, and it stuck until something else happened.

One night I had a dream. I was standing in a bathroom in my old high school in Sandy. It had not been cleaned in decades. There were 3-foot piles of, well, crap everywhere and the place stunk. I was looking in a mirror at myself. In my reflection, I was wearing a hard and static mask that looked like a white skull. Suddenly the mask along the jaw line cracked and fell off revealing my face underneath. Music started to play. I knew the song; it was by George Strait, the hit single that he released in 2011. I started to sing and dance. This was so good that it could have been choreographed on Broadway. I burst out of the disgusting bathroom into an only slightly less disgusting hallway. All the way through the first verse I was strutting down the hallway waving to people. On the down beat of the start of the chorus I started sliding down the hallway like I was skating. By the time I got to the end of the chorus I was at the junction of the hallway with the main lobby near the cafeteria. At the start of the second verse I turned a perfect 90 degrees and started strutting down the way in front of the cafeteria towards the main door of the school. As I walked past the cafeteria I watched as the people there were eating what I am guessing was the same stuff that was in the bathroom—that caused me to quicken my pace. I reached the statue in front of the main door at the last line of the second verse. That line is, "bring on anything." As soon as I said it I flipped around and flipped off the entire school. I then turned around and I burst through the main doors and into the outside world singing the chorus to the song the whole time.

I was on a high for two full days.

The meaning of the dream is this. Do you remember my second grade teacher Mrs. J.? Because of the abuse I suffered from her and the compounded issues I had during the rest of my childhood, I put on a mask of sorts in order to hide my true feelings and motives and personality. I was "putting on a brave face" so that I could lessen the impact of what I was feeling. I didn't even know that I was doing it. It took 20 years before I was able to take it off. When I woke up I could actually feel the mask on my face due to the contrast between it and my regular face. Over the next 3 days following the dream, I was able to remove the rest of the mask with meditation all the while enjoying the release of my natural face.

As for the setting in the high school…Jordan was in many ways the epitome of dashed dreams for me. I had such expectations for that place, and when they were not met for reasons that were either my fault or the fault of the micro society that was high school, my life was poisoned for years to come. Of course high school is supposed to be hard, but that hardness should not be a result of race, or religion, or even family name. If you don't like a person then leave them alone; don't make their life worse. It's probably bad enough without you compounding the suffering.

My goal as far as life and school is concerned, is to get through it and become the best doctor that this world has ever seen. In fact I want to honor BDK and surpass him in both skill and knowledge. It is said that if a student can surpass his teacher and work in the way that his teacher had intended, then his teacher has succeeded. BDK has done a great deal for me, I owe it to him.

I also spend a lot of my time writing, obviously. This is not the only thing that I have written. I have a few scripts that are in various stages of completion including an epic that is ready to either be edited or optioned. If you're interested, let me know. I have a comedy that is based loosely on my teenage years. I am even re-writing a piece of classic literature and setting it in the modern day. I enjoy writing, even if what I write doesn't sell there is just something about putting your thoughts down on paper and at least hoping that somebody will someday read and enjoy them.

I thank all the people that have helped me, especially during this latest chapter in my life. One man in particular who is the Doctoral Director at Emperor's has helped me tremendously. After I had purged the negativity from my Liver I sat down with him to learn how to use emotion properly. Basically what he told me was it is not something that can be learned or taught. It is instead something that every human being is able to do, just like breathing. All that I needed to do was look inside my heart to find what I already knew how to do. It took me 2 hours and a sandwich to figure out that was what he was saying to me that day. Thanks to that talk I was able to make peace with my emotions and actually use them the way that they were intended to be used. I have undone the damage that was done to me by the Church and the misguided efforts of my mother and father. I can now feel emotions and I feel them properly.

As I finish writing I look back on all that I have written on my life, as short as it has been. Despite the fact that I am now drowning in debt and I will probably never get out of it, this is the best my life has been. Believe it or not I'm happy, because I am the me that I want to be. I'm doing things that my family would never have ever thought I could do. I live in a city that I never thought I would live in. I am studying and practicing my passion. I am not stuck in a dead-end job chained to a desk somewhere. Every day that I look at this new life of mine I am amazed at what has happened.

Now just a few last parting things. No matter what, never give up. If you are supposed to do it, then you will be able to do it. In Taoism good and evil don't technically exist. This philosophy tells you to be the best at whatever you are whether you are a street sweeper, a drunk, or just a good person trying to survive. My goal in writing this book is for people who are going through what I have gone through to see my mistakes and try to change before going through the worst of it. Then if you are in the worst of it, I wanted this to serve as a ray of light in the darkness of the mind. In the end we are all the same, just as we are at the beginning. The middle is nothing more than a lie. Be who you are, not who you think you should be. Find a reason to laugh every day, and that reason cannot be at the expense of someone else. Just look around this world is hilarious. Listen more than talk. And please love everyone for no reason.

www.ingramcontent.com/pod-product-compliance
Lightning Source LLC
Chambersburg PA
CBHW061428040426
42450CB00007B/944
9780578110721